T0157467

TRULY DELIVERED

TRULY DELIVERED

SEEING MYSELF IN HIS IMAGE

Jennifer P. Byfield

TRUE DIRECTIONS
AN AFFILIATE OF TARCHER BOOKS

TRULY DELIVERED
SEEING MYSELF IN HIS IMAGE

Copyright © 2015 Jennifer P. Byfield.

All rights reserved. No part of this book may be used or reproduced by any means, graphic, electronic, or mechanical, including photocopying, recording, taping or by any information storage retrieval system without the written permission of the publisher except in the case of brief quotations embodied in critical articles and reviews.

The views expressed in this work are solely those of the author and do not necessarily reflect the views of the publisher, and the publisher hereby disclaims any responsibility for them.

iUniverse books may be ordered through booksellers or by contacting:

iUniverse
1663 Liberty Drive
Bloomington, IN 47403
www.iuniverse.com
1-800-Authors (1-800-288-4677)

Because of the dynamic nature of the Internet, any web addresses or links contained in this book may have changed since publication and may no longer be valid.

Any people depicted in stock imagery provided by Thinkstock are models, and such images are being used for illustrative purposes only. Certain stock imagery © Thinkstock.

ISBN: 978-1-4917-6520-3 (sc)
ISBN: 978-1-4917-6519-7 (e)

Print information available on the last page.

iUniverse rev. date: 5/4/2015

This book is dedicated to Winston and Bethune Vaz,
who have given me a solid foundation by raising
me to give honour and respect to my Creator. It is through
their parenting that I was able to make the wisest choice,
when I accepted the salvation of Jesus Christ.

To my husband, Bishop Nathan Byfield, whom I thank
for his help and support in publishing this book.

To my children, Darren and Loveive.

Words from the Author

From the time I could understand as a child, the Word of God was presented to me. I grew up in a religious home, where we were required to be in the house of God every time the doors were open for service. There were no exceptions to the rule, unless I was ill. In my limited understanding, I grew to love it, simply because of the gathering. I looked forward to the excitement of it all and seeing those whose company I cherished.

Although I participated in the Bible studies and heard many sermons, most of what remained inside of me were the songs we used to sing. At the time, I didn't realize just how powerful a song is. Learning that Jesus loves me, Jesus is a friend like no other, and Jesus saves—all in song—was useful in laying my spiritual foundation.

As I became older, I grew more into listening to God's Word taught by my Sunday school teachers, words from my pastor, and, more importantly, words from my own parents. In my middle teenage years, I began to stray into the jungle world that was calling me out from my safety net of salvation. Before I knew it, I was deep into the wild, and the words and songs that were once my guiding light became faint. But in the late nights, when all was quiet and still, I yearned for what was. I felt very far away from home and was uncertain how I would get back there. I felt very lost, alone and unsure of my direction. Funny thing, though—it was as though there was a mark on me that everyone could see—except me.

Every so often, I would come across someone who was bold enough to say, "You do not belong here; you are not one of us." I was trying to blend in, go with the flow, but it became overwhelming for me, and I began to cry out for my friend like no other, the one who loves me and the one who saves. One day, while strolling through the shopping mall, I heard someone call out my name, and I stopped to talk with her. She had recognized me from the church we both attended when I was a child. In fact, she was a deacon's daughter.

She asked me about my place of worship, as if it were a mandatory thing. She seemed strong and reassured and discerning enough to see I was clearly off my path. She did not hesitate to invite me to her place of worship; I could tell she was excited to help the poor lost sheep find her way home. I accepted her invitation and attended the service, and sure enough, it felt just like home again. This had nothing to do with the people or the place, but rather the familiar words and songs. I was so thirsty for God that when they offered water baptism, I did it without delay.

As I began to read God's Word, it opened my eyes to things I never knew were there. The more I read, the more I saw. I felt rebuked, corrected, ashamed, incomplete, but I also felt loved, hopeful, reassured and so much more. I was being cleansed, healed and delivered. I began to see myself as God would have me be— what others were seeing and I couldn't—until I could look into the mirror. God's Word was, is and always will be the mirror that shows our true reflection.

Without this mirror, you will have no understanding of who you are or, more importantly, who God is. Since we are made in his image, it is in our best interest to know what he looks like. You may be having this same experience I have shared with you. Your only solution is to get to a mirror and see for yourself. The image of God is not merely a figure but the characteristics of one who is holy, pure and true. There is something very powerful about his image that causes the old Adamic nature of sin to crumble. Although we can never know this supreme spiritual being in his entirety while we are in this earthly body, he has shown us enough to make us better prepared for a face-to-face, up-close-and-personal encounter with him.

I pray that this book will be a source of inspiration and help for you and that whatever you receive, you will share it with others. Always keep in mind that God has made us into a blessing, that we can be a blessing to others in return.

Preface

Examining Oneself
Truly Delivered

*T*his book is written for believers who desire to live a more fulfilling life as children of God. It is also for those sitting on the fence, unable to make up their minds which side they are on. As a born-again child of God, I have had the opportunity to experience both sides. Before I was saved, quite naturally I must have been a sinner.

Living a sinful life is completely different from being saved. Many people, through dishonesty, will not admit to enjoying their lives as sinners, but I did enjoy it, because like many people, I was under the illusion that sin is sweet. By now, everyone has figured out that the things that are no good for you always look the best, feel the best, and taste the best—although it is our sinful nature that gives us this perception.

Sin makes everything that is bad for you seem like the best, so it becomes irresistible. This is why you cannot be saved from sin unless you have consciously chosen to no longer partake of sinful things; it is a matter of choice. You have to decide who or what you love more: sin or salvation, God or the devil. Some people want to have both, but you cannot.

I often hear people say, "It's hard to make the change." It's only hard because you love sin more. The love of God has not yet entered your heart. It is true that love conquers. When the love of God came into my heart, I instantly became uninterested in immoral things. The change in me became apparent, so much so that my friends were in total disbelief. They couldn't understand how I had transformed, literally overnight. But salvation is sudden; it doesn't take years for you to receive it, once your heart is ready. That's the miracle of salvation. The only thing most people have not yet realized is that you have a part to play in maintaining your miracle. Like everything else we possess, without caring for our miracles, they will be of very little use to us eventually. This I had to learn.

Although I have received salvation, and it brought about a sudden change in my life, I was unsure of what to do next. I know gathering with people of like minds was part of it. Praying and reading God's Word are steps in maintenance; but how do I stop my struggle with sin, seeing that it was paying me a daily visit, coercing me to engage in the same immoral lifestyle I used to enjoy? There were days when the temptation was so great, I wasn't able to reach out to the Lord. I simply wasn't strong enough yet. There were days when sin caused me to question whether I was truly saved.

If you examine the Word of God, you will see that more times than not, Jesus gave a charge to the people for whom he performed miracles, that they should keep away from that which had them bound. Staying away from the very things that held you captive in sin is your first step in securing your miracle. The second thing you need to do is stay very close to the one from whom you've received your miracle. Third, you need to heed the words of the keeper of miracles.

Sin is designed to keep us away from our miracles, in order to have victory over us. We have to keep the Word of God in our hearts. "Thy word have I hid in mine heart that I might not sin against thee" (Psalm 119:11). After reading this passage, I began to realize that for me to live a victorious life over sin I have to get the Word of God out of my head and into my heart. As I practiced doing this, I noticed that my struggle between sin and salvation became less, and my appetite for sin decreased. I began to see the promises and the benefits of salvation manifesting in my life. (See Psalm 1)

I have been inspired by the Holy Spirit to write this book of deliverance to help those who struggle with this same problem. You will notice that throughout this book, references to various Scriptures have been made, to give clarity of my findings to the reader. All Scriptures have been taken from the King James Version of the Bible; for more clarity, you can use the New International Version.

The book of Exodus was used as a base in all chapters, as Exodus means "going out," as in leaving. God's people left a place of sin and spiritual barrenness, to go to a place where they could better serve God. Exodus represents deliverance for God's people. It is my desire that this book will be a source of deliverance for the godly, the ungodly and the sinners. Sin destroys people's lives; though tempting, enticing and enjoyable, it may be more like eating your favorite food laced with arsenic.

In Hosea 4:6, God said, "my people are destroyed for lack of knowledge," clearly knowledge of his Word.

Sadly, not many people who say they are saved take time out to know or understand God's Word and therefore find themselves constantly reverting back to their own sinful ways. In conclusion, they can never seem to grow past the first two stages of being saved: repentance and water baptism. People need to know there are higher heights and deeper depths in God that can only be reached by knowing, understanding and obeying his Word.

Contents

Introduction

*T*hroughout my life, I have not yet found anything as gratifying as salvation—and it's free. Go figure. Of course, neither have I met anyone who wasn't sceptical or suspicious of anything that had the word *free* attached to it—myself included; but seriously, can you really blame us? We live in a world that is so corrupt that it's hard to believe when anything is for real. We live in a world full of lies and deception, a world where the wicked fabricate the truth to catch people.

Every time you turn on the television, you hear some kind of a lie to convince you to buy some product by any means necessary. Then there are the local retailers tricking you into buying their products through false advertising like buy-one-get-one-free schemes, when the truth is they have already combined the price for two into one. Of course, it is no surprise that politicians are lying to us and making false promises to get our votes; so-called professionals, with their advanced degrees, lie to us in order to line their pockets. I call them professional thieves.

Although none of these things should ever be accepted, I believe the worst deception is that which comes through the people you love and trust the most. This can burn you pretty badly, but we need to face the fire sometimes. As people who profess to be disciples of Jesus Christ, we have certainly managed to give the world a bad impression of him. I once heard a preacher make the sad statement, "Christians are liars."

When we—the people of God, who are supposed to be the mirror image of a God who is truth and love—fail to represent, the statement is quite understandable. We cannot expect anything better from a world of sinners, when we ourselves aren't setting any example for them to follow. We are the light of the world.

It is more devastating that we are sometimes not liars deliberately but through our lack of knowledge of God's Word. Still you are without excuse because it is your responsibility to acquaint yourself with God's Word. Whether you are able to read or not, you have the ability to listen. If you are able to see or hear and understand, then you are obligated to do so.

How many times have you heard a sinner say, "Church people are liars"? For me, it's enough times to lose count. Our lying ways have given them a reason to disbelieve God's Word. When we say that God has changed us, yet we continue to do the things the world recognizes as a part of them, then we are seen as liars. Second Corinthians 5:17 says, "therefore if any man is in Christ, he is a new creature: old things are passed away; behold all things are become new." The Word of God did not say *perfect;* it said *new.* Don't go around professing that you are new in Christ when you are hanging out with sinners and doing what they do. The beauty of salvation is the transformation.

This is why it says in Romans 12:2, "be not conformed to this world: but be ye transformed by the renewing of your mind." No human mind that is accustomed to sinning can be transformed into thinking righteously without the Word of God. You're not hiding, just because you get dressed up and go into the house of God with the people of God; in secret, you are still doing the things that are contrary to God's Word. We may be able to fool man, but God knows you are a liar. You cannot be new without the Word; it's just not possible. Sin has broken you, and no one knows how to fix you better than the one who made you.

"Can the Ethiopian change his skin; or the leopard his spots? Then may he also do what is good that are accustomed to do evil" (Jeremiah13:23). You need God to fix you. Stop pretending you're all right when you are not.

One thing I find impressive about substance-abuse rehabilitation clinics is their refusal to help any person with a problem who isn't willing to admit the truth about his or her situation. It is hard to help anyone who cannot recognize the need for help. The truth is, you wouldn't need to go to rehab anyhow if you just go to God's Word.

Often we end up paying for help we could receive if we had just given God the first chance. John 8:32 says, "you shall know the truth and the truth shall make you free." So in fact, you can say it is not getting with man's program that helps you but knowing and admitting the truth. Our own ideas are blocking us from receiving God's Word. It's not what we think we should do that helps us; it is doing what God requires of us.

Many times, through laziness we seek out quick fixes, instead of going to the Word. This only makes it harder to build the relationship God desires with us. Over the years, I've watched the people of God develop a trend. They go anywhere, near or far, for a prophet—real or fake—to lay hands on them and deliver them from their troubles or whatever they may be lacking. Many times we make liars out of them by expecting them to tell us what they do not know or help us when they can't.

Although there is nothing wrong with hands being laid on us for our healing or deliverance, we are never truly delivered until we walk in obedience to God's Word. We cannot have unbelievers thinking that God's kingdom is without rules and principles; that we can live any careless way and still receive the blessing of the Lord. Many times, people come to the house of the Lord to receive prayer to see them through hard times. After their hard times have passed, they no longer have use for the house or the prayer.

I have attended many so-called deliverance services where people come to be free from unclean spirits. They will leave claiming to be delivered, yet they are still hateful, covetous and angry. We need to do what the Word says, so we are not only delivered for one day but are walking in our deliverance. I don't want to be an accuser, especially not a false one, so I will just say that I hope leaders are telling people what is truth.

The truth is really that there is no true deliverance without doing what the Word says. Our real prayer for each other should be that we become doers of God's Word and not just hearers only. "If we are hearers of the word only and not doers, we are deceiving our own selves" (James 1:22). Perhaps we need to redefine *deliverance.* Many people seek deliverance without understanding what it is or more importantly what they need to be delivered from and why.

Deliverance is simply freedom, otherwise known as salvation. We need to be delivered from evil, as Jesus taught his disciples in Matthew 6. Evil in us or around us is a destructive force, purposed to prevent us from true freedom. When you've truly received salvation and begin to walk in it, you will not need anyone to tell you when and if you are delivered. "If the son therefore shall make you free, you are free indeed" (John 8:36). You should know for yourself if Jesus Christ is living inside you; if not him, then who?

There is a simple song we are used to singing, but we miss the message it brings: "When Jesus comes, the tempter's power is broken. When Jesus comes, all tears are wiped away. He takes your gloom and fills your life with glory, for all is changed when Jesus comes to stay." Is Jesus truly living in your heart? Examine yourself to see whether or not he is there.

When Jesus comes, we will be perfected in love. "Perfect love casts out fear" (1 John 4:18). When Jesus comes, we will be free from the fears to which evil has had us bound; free to love and be loved. Fear is the incubator for every work of evil. As long as fear is within you, you will always feel undelivered.

You will know when a person has truly received deliverance. Every other bit of what God has to offer is of interest to them. He is not just there for their convenience, like a drug dealer to supply their next hit. He will become their saviour, the one on whom they depend to make them clean and whole again. They are not afraid to trust him with their lives.

We need the world to start believing us. For this to happen, we have to start manifesting the Word, and for *that* to happen, we have to receive it, believe and do it. This is very important; before we can convince the world, we have to first practice the Word on each other as children of God. No more lying to each other.

One very serious lie that we tell before God, to ourselves and to others, is that we love God's people, when in fact we hate them. We really need to work on that. Whoever hates his brother is a murderer, and you know that no murderer hath eternal life abiding in him (1 John 3:15). It goes on to say in verse 18, "let us not love in word, neither in tongue; but in deed and truth."

The mouth was made to speak, but sometimes we should refrain from speaking unless we are speaking the truth in love. Love is something that will be tested to prove it. When God said he loved us, not only did he say it, he proved it by giving his only Son to die for our sins. Love is not found in words but in actions. Jesus said, "By this shall all men know that you are my disciples, if you have Love one toward another." (John 13:35)

If we can't convince our own brothers and sisters of the love of Christ within us, how then will the world believe when we tell them Jesus loves them? We ourselves have not yet received it for ourselves. The world is suffering a great need for salvation, yet many are having a hard time believing that it's available to them free of cost, because the ones who have already gotten it are trying to sell it to them.

Salvation is not only free; there is much more to it yet to be discovered. It is a popular belief that there is no such thing as "free." Some also say that if by chance you do get something for free, it's never any good. Contrary to popular belief, not only is salvation free, it is absolutely the greatest thing. Many people of

God still aren't able to say this, because they have not opened their gift since the time they have received it. They only got it because it was free, but they have shown no excitement about the package, let alone what's on the inside.

So here you have a gift that will help you to live better, love better, see better, hear better, feel better; something that will make you kinder, stronger, healthier, prettier—but you don't know because you haven't taken the time to open it. It's been one year, five years, even ten years now since you've received salvation, and no one can see the difference because you have not taken advantage of what's inside. Start today!

Chapter 1

You're Different

*I*f you are not of light, you are of darkness; if you are not of good, you are of evil. There is no in-between, so do not be fooled by the proverbial shades of gray. There are no shades of gray with Almighty God. The world is divided for you to choose: God's way or not. In Exodus 11:7, God said to Moses, "but against any of the children of Israel shall not a dog move his tongue, against man or beast: that ye may know how that the Lord doth put a difference between the Egyptians and Israel."

The world must see the difference in us as the children of God. In John 17:16, Jesus said, "they are not of the world, even as I am not of the world," referring to those who belong to him. The world represents darkness, while Jesus Christ represents light. How then can we be followers of Christ and want to be a part of the very thing he's taken us out of? In Matthew 5:14, Jesus again taught his disciples about kingdom living and the things that should identify them as children of God. He said, "Ye are the light of the world. A city that is set on a hill cannot be hid." In verse 15, he said, "neither do men light a candle and put it under a bushel, but on a candlestick, and it gives light unto all that are in the house." He further went on in verse 16 to say, "Let your light so shine before men; that they may see your good works, and glorify your father which is in heaven." Jesus' time on earth

1

was spent glorifying his Father. He didn't just preach it; he lived it. That's what separated him from the world. He was different; he spoke his Father's language, and so must we also speak that same language of love, forgiveness, repentance, healing, deliverance, mercy, joy, peace, judgement and justice.

The world's way of doing things is exactly what Jesus warned us about. He proved to us that we do not have to be enticed by worldly pleasures when he rejected Satan's offer in Matthew 4:8–10. He was not about to bow down and worship Satan for what belongs to his Father. How many of us have already traded our souls for some false promise from Satan? Psalm 24:1–2 declares "the earth is the Lord's and the fullness thereof; the world and they that dwell therein. For, he hath founded it upon the seas and established it upon the floods."

Don't fall for the devil's tricks of enticing you with what already belongs to you. The world should be enticed by the things of God, not the other way around. We are supposed to be inviting them to come into the light, not for us to go into the darkness. God has called us to make a difference, and he is not accepting mediocrity. It's either him or the world; you must choose. You cannot be with God and the world at the same time. It's not possible. So decide which side you're on, and stop playing with your life. *You are different!*

Beautiful Garment

Have you ever stopped to consider the garments you wear? As I read through Exodus 28, it occurred to me that we take the clothing we wear for granted, especially as ministers, and this should not be. In order for Aaron and his sons to minister before the Lord, they were properly attired, compliments of the anointed fashion industry. It doesn't seem as if anyone shops there anymore; we have fallen subject to the world's way of dressing and have taken up their trends.

God's designs are no longer appealing to many who say they are kingdom children. We should consider that God does nothing without a purpose. "Thou shall make holy garments for Aaron thy brother for glory and for beauty" (Exodus 28:2). Ministering to God's people is a representation of him, and it should be taken seriously. In verse 3, instructions were given to wise people to make Aaron's clothing.

We have a lot of foolish people making clothes today, and a lot of foolish people buying them. I realize that the labels on our clothing sometimes tell us the hearts and minds of the people who are designing them. For instance, there is a clothing label called Seduction, so if you are planning to seduce someone with your garments, it is the perfect outfit. Let us wake up and become more conscious of what we are doing.

Everything we do as people of God is reflected on him. In ways we haven't considered, we can turn his glory into shame. The world should be following *our* fashion trend, not the other way around. Because of our own lust for worldly things, we have twisted the very Word of God to feel comfortable in fulfilling our own desires.

We have comforted ourselves with Joel 2:13, which says, "rend your heart and not your garments." We are always looking for loopholes to rebel and disobey God. Jesus Christ is Lord over all things and is simply saying, "follow my way of doing things." But we don't want God's way; we want our way. No! You can't dress any way you want as children of God. We really need to become more conscious of how we dress.

Although the Lord requires the cleanliness of your heart above all, he is also expecting our garments to also make a statement to the world; we are different, after all. I do agree with you: no beautiful garment is going to make your heart clean; but on the flip side, there is something to be said about a clean heart wearing beautiful garments. Esther 5:1–2 is a perfect demonstration of how a pure heart coupled with beautiful garments can have a profound effect on those who look upon you. Queen Esther went before the Lord for three days in consecration and then put on her royal apparel to go before the king. When his eyes beheld her, he was unable to resist her, to the point of granting her request by giving her up to half his kingdom.

Let's get back to our heritage. First Peter 2:9 tells us who we are, and we should walk in that. We are a chosen generation, a royal priesthood, a holy nation, a peculiar people, that we should show forth the praises of him who has called us out of darkness into his marvellous light.

It is a shame to see the way some women attire themselves coming to the house of the Lord; there is nothing left to the imagination. Some of the outfits are so tight, you can see all their body parts and lingerie, outfits so short up to their midthigh, and they have no shame of it. Sometimes it is done deliberately to seduce both leaders and members they may have set their sights on.

It is so much more important to see men who are made to be an example of the attributes of God following instead of leading by wearing these clinging garments they think will be appealing to the women. I for one am not impressed; I still believe in mystery and leaving something to the imagination.

What is more disturbing is to see women ministers standing before the congregation in outfits so short, you can see their thighs. God forbid they should bend down to pick something up! I've seen praise and worship leaders who take no pride in their presentation to the people. Their outfits are so outrageous, it is distracting. You have to keep your eyes closed in worship to not be offended. There are male pastors whose outfits are so tight, they look more like wrestlers and football players than men of God who are there to set an example.

I know you're thinking that God doesn't look at our outward appearance, and you are right according to 2 Samuel 16:7, but does it mean that we can still dress any way we please, to stand before God's people? No! It doesn't. God is saying that because of our human limitations and boundaries, we are incapable of seeing the true nature of a person's heart without God's help, so sometimes we tend to judge the character of people wrongly.

You may be someone whose outfit is so provocative now that I may be offended, but God sees something great in you. You may be someone whose outfit is sweeping the floor, and I have to wonder about your body size underneath all that material, but you are a wolf in sheep's clothing.

What am I saying? Everything we do as children of God should bring glory to God. We bring glory to God by our ways and our actions demonstrated to people. People will come to believe in God through our behaviour, and they can also turn away from him through our behaviour. As a child of God, you should care how you are seen by people. Don't dress to follow a trend; set an example and be a leader.

Believe it or not, this is another way the devil is tricking you to turn God's glory into shame. We are the glory of God. If you are truly living for the Lord, everything you do should reflect that. You can be attractive without wearing something short, tight and provocative. Will you dare to be different for the glory of God?

Take Off Your Ornaments

For the Lord had said unto Moses, "say unto the children of Israel, you are a stiff-necked people: I will come up into the midst of thee in a moment, and consume thee; therefore now put off thy ornaments from thee, that I may know what to do unto thee. So the children of Israel stripped themselves of their ornaments by the Mount Ho'-reb" (Exodus 33:5–6). Where has our shame gone? No one wears the face of shame anymore.

Sometimes it seems as if our conscience is gone. We have not changed from being stiff-necked. We still fight against God every day and oppose his Word, yet there is no sense of remorse for our behaviour. It seems as if we don't need to have God's approval anymore. Our attitude seems to say, "Thanks for dying for my sins. Now I am free to do whatever I want; now leave me alone." But God is still recording our stiff-necked ways, and he is still angry every time we rebel against him, and he is still expecting us to take off our ornaments until he decides what to do about our bad behaviour.

Many people, saved and unsaved, are still trying to understand why God would refer to King David as being a man after his own heart, but it's not hard to understand if you know the heart of God. Loving, caring, compassionate, longsuffering, gentle, kind, gracious, slow to anger, plenteous in mercy is our God. He is a Father who loves his children and wants the best for them.

Our qualities should match up with our Father's, and you could never be happy if he is not. Yes, King David was an adulterer, a killer, a liar, and much more I'm sure, but when he found out that his Father was not at all pleased with his bad behaviour, he too stripped himself of his ornaments and threw himself down in humility before him until his Father made a decision what to do with him (2 Samuel 11–13).

God's heart is one of humility. That's why in Psalm 51:16–18, David could write, "for thou desires not sacrifice; else would I give it: thou delights not in burnt offering. The sacrifices of God are a broken spirit: a broken and a contrite heart, O! God, thou will not despise. Do good, in thy good pleasure unto Zion: build thou the walls of Jerusalem."

The walls of our spiritual Jerusalem today have been broken down because of our lack of repentance, and if we expect God to build them up again, which only he can, we need to throw off our ornaments and prostrate before our Father in humility of heart.

One of the greatest acts of repentance is recorded in the book of Jonah. Jonah began to enter into the city, a day's journey, and he cried and said, "Yet forty days, and Nineveh shall be overthrown."

So the people of Nineveh believed God, and proclaimed a fast, putting on sackcloth, from the greatest of them even to the least of them. For word came unto the king of Nineveh, and he arose from his throne, and he laid his robe from him and covered him with sackcloth and sat in ashes. He caused it to be proclaimed and published throughout Nineveh by the decree of the king and his nobles, saying, "Let neither man nor beast, herd nor flock, taste any thing: let them not feed, nor drink water: but let man and beast be covered with sackcloth, and cry mightily unto God: yea, let them turn everyone from his evil way, and from the violence that is in their hands. Who can tell if God will turn and repent, and turn from his fierce anger that we perish not?" God saw their works, that they turned from their evil way, and God repented of the evil that he had said that he would do unto them, and he did it not.

The people of Nineveh did not know the true and living God as we do, yet with one warning of repentance, they did not hesitate. How much more is required of us who receive the repentance message every day? In Matthew 12, the scribes and the Pharisees asked Jesus for a sign to believe that they should turn from their wicked ways; but Jesus answered and said unto them, "An evil and adulterous generation seeks after a sign; and there shall no sign be given to it, but the sign of the prophet Jonas." The men of Nineveh shall rise in judgement with this generation and shall condemn it because they repented at the preaching of Jonas; and behold a greater than Jonas is here. Stop playing games with God; you know where you've come up short. Do yourself a favor and repent.

> Behold, I am vile; what shall I answer thee?
> I will lay mine hand upon my mouth.
> —Job 40:4

Chapter 2

Get Sanctified

*I*t's time to get sanctified, people. The Lord is coming back for his church, and he is coming back to find it without spots or wrinkles. In Exodus 19:10, the Lord said unto Moses, "Go unto the people and sanctify them today and tomorrow, and let them wash their clothes."

We have certainly been playing around, playing in all sorts of mud and dirt. After all, that's what children do. But we're now living in a time when the Lord is saying, *No more playing. Enough is enough; it's late in the evening, and supper is almost ready.* I mean, if we truly were interested in what's on the menu, we would run inside. Not only that; when Daddy says come in, he means it. Otherwise someone is in trouble.

If you are feeling so big and grown up with your big titles, don't bother. You're not above him scolding you; no one is exempt from this command. In Exodus 19:22, the Lord told Moses, "let the Priests also, which come near to the Lord, sanctify themselves, lest the Lord break forth upon them." Many of us are under the impression that we can play around as much as we want, because we are called by the name of Jesus, and all will be well.

Here's a wake-up for you: there is a call for repentance, and it's time we get to the place of sanctification and consecration. Why should you be allowed to dine at the royal table, looking like some rebel? God wants you to know the time has been far spent. I know this is a loud, strong statement. Don't worry; I'm not singling you out. It includes me as well. Didn't you hear? *Everyone,* The whole five-fold, apostles, prophets, evangelists, pastors, teachers, from the greatest to the least—get started. Don't look so high and mighty; just obey for once.

In that dispensation, God spoke of not only the hearts of the people but also their literal garments. In this time, although it is wonderful to dress up in our nice white suits and dresses, God is not impressed without the cleanliness of your heart and hands. That's how it was then and how it is now.

In Jewish custom, mourners tear their garments in the place where their heart is located, to symbolize how broken their hearts were for the loved ones they mourned. However, in Joel 2:13, the prophet rebuked them to tear their hearts and not their garments, meaning they should be more concerned with the condition of their hearts and not mere symbolism.

Regardless of what your mouth may say and your body may do, God is most impressed with a genuinely repentant heart. Psalm 24:3–5 asked and answered, "who shall ascend into the hill of the Lord? Or who shall stand in his holy place? He that has clean hands and pure hearts, he have not lifted up his soul unto vanity, nor sworn deceitfully. He shall receive the blessing from the Lord, and righteousness from the God of his salvation."

It's time we align ourselves with the Word of God. Ephesians 5:15 admonishes, "see then that you walk circumspectly, not as fools; but as wise, redeeming the time; because they are evil." The million-dollar question is, how will we survive? Unless we sanctify ourselves and walk in it, we cannot make it. Titus 3:3 says, "we ourselves, also were sometimes foolish, disobedient, deceived, serving diver's lusts and pleasures, living in malice and envy, hateful and hating one another." Let us not continue in these ways but be sanctified and prepared for the return of our King.

The Lord's Side

Then Moses stood in the gate of the camp and said, "Who is on the Lord's side? Let him come unto me," and all the sons of Levi gathered themselves together unto him (Exodus 32:26). Moses was not addressing non-believers; he was talking to the people of God because their behaviour was not in conjunction with God's ways. Don't think anything has changed.

You still have people today who know who God is but deny his power. They appear as though they are part of the church, but they are not. They have not truly made a solid commitment to follow the Lord. They are not on his side. Jesus made this perfectly clear in Matthew 7:21. "Not everyone that says Lord, Lord, shall enter into the kingdom of heaven, but he that does the will of his father which is in heaven."

Not everyone is willing to be obedient to God's will. It doesn't always fit into our lifestyles; but once again, we are right back in Exodus 32, and the offer still stands. If you are truly on the Lord's side, you have to make a quick decision now. It's a matter of life and death. Will you be counted among the Levites? You can't afford to be caught in your clothes of rebellion.

When Moses went away to seek the Lord for his commandments, the people took it upon themselves to create a God for them to worship. Their hearts were not on the Lord. In spite of all the Lord had done for them, they could not revere him as their God. They did not trust him to come through for them; instead they trusted in their vanity.

God wasn't pleased then, and he certainly is not pleased now, just as the people waited for Moses to return, so are we now waiting for Jesus Christ to return. Matthew 24:42 says, "watch therefore: for you know not what hour your Lord will come." But know this: if the good man of the house had known in what hour the thief would come, he would have watched and would not have suffered his house to be broken up. Therefore be ye also ready: for in such an hour as he think not the son of man comes.

Who then is the faithful and wise servant, whom his lord has made ruler over his household, to give them meat in due season? Blessed is that servant, whom his lord, when he comes, shall find so doing. Verily I say unto you that he shall make him ruler over all his goods. But if that evil servant shall say in his heart, *my lord delays his coming,* and shall begin to smite his fellow servants and to eat and drink with the drunken, the lord of that servant shall come in a day when he looks not for him, and in an hour that he is not aware of and shall cut him asunder and appoint him his portion with the hypocrites. There shall be weeping and gnashing of teeth.

The Lord already knows that we have all sinned and come short of his glory, but he will not tolerate our hypocrisies in pretending that our hearts are toward him, when we are truly worshipping another god. What we yield ourselves to becomes our master. No matter how long our Lord takes to return, we should remain faithful to him, and we will in no way lose our reward. If you have already made the Lord your choice, don't let anything separate you from him. Be sure you are under the same persuasion the apostle Paul speaks of in Romans 8.

Chapter 3

Keeping God's Commandments

*E*xodus 40 makes reference to Moses doing as the Lord commanded him ten times. I believe the author is calling to our attention how important it is for us to follow God's commandments. Moses was faithful in all that the Lord had told him to do, and we should be no different. God is counting on us to be exactly that: faithful. Because we are under the law of grace, we should not practice being sloppy with God's commandments.

Contrary to what you may be thinking, whoever you are, not all commandments have been abolished or adjusted to suit your way of life. They are still very much effective, and we are expected to uphold them.

Keeping God's commandments is obviously very important for us to do, which is why the fight is so great for us *not* to uphold them. Revelation 12:17 tells us of the Dragon (Satan) being angry with the woman and going to make war with the remnant of her seed, which keep the commandments of God and have the testimony of Jesus Christ.

Just as the old Dragon is fighting for us not to keep the commandments of God, we should fight all the more to keep them. In Matthew 5:17-19, Jesus said, "think not that I am come to destroy the Law or the Prophets; I am not come to destroy but to fulfill, for verily I say unto you, till heaven and earth pass, one jot or one tittle shall in no wise pass away from the Law, till all be fulfilled. Whosoever therefore shall break one of these lease commandments and shall teach men so, he shall be called the least in the kingdom of heaven; but whosoever shall do and teach them, the same shall be called great in the kingdom of heaven."

Jesus Christ walked in fulfilling the commandments given by the Father, and so should we follow accordingly. We wonder why things can't seem to fall in our favour, being followers of Jesus Christ. We cannot expect God to work on our behalf if we don't believe in his laws. Psalm 103:17–18 says, "but the mercy of the Lord is everlasting to everlasting upon them that fear him and his righteousness unto children's, children, to such as keep his covenant, and to those that remember his commandments to do them." Psalm 119:113 says, "depart from me ye evildoers for I will keep the commandments of my God"; 119:151 says, "thou art near, O Lord; and all thy commandments are truth."

The truth does not change for us. Moses followed all of God's commandments; because he believed God, he knew the character of God enough to know that God's commandments were in the best interest of his people. You cannot choose which commandments to keep and which to throw away. Every kingdom or government is governed by laws, which the people are expected to follow. If we break any law, there are consequences, and we are held accountable. Consider, then, that you are dealing with a God who is the government of the entire universe. It is silly for us to think we can negotiate on the rules and regulations he has set to keep order in it.

There are two different types of laws the Bible speaks of. The two laws contrasted; the moral laws, which are the royal verses, and the ceremonial laws (sacrificial). The moral laws or *mishpatim* relate to justice and judgement and are said to be based upon God's holy nature, which makes them holy, just, and unchanging.

Their purpose is to promote the welfare of those who obey. These commandments, whose reason is obvious, and the benefit of their fulfillment in the world are known, such as the prohibition of theft and murder and the commandment to respect parents.

The moral laws were given by God, who is our King; therefore, they are royal. The law is intended to guide us into right doing. It is a roadmap to the truth and carries no punishment. These laws were spoken by God (Deuteronomy 4:12).

They were written by him on tables of stone (Exodus 24:12). They are right, true, and good (Nehemiah 9:13), which if a man do, he shall live in them (Ezekiel 20:11). It is the perfect law (Psalm 19:7). "Christ did not come to destroy it" (Matthew 5:17); he came to "magnify" it and make it "honourable" (Isaiah 42:21).

The ceremonial laws are called *hukkim* or *chuqqah* in Hebrew, which literally means "custom of the nation." The ceremonial law (sacrificial) was given by Moses for the people. It was added because of the people's transgressions against the moral laws. Therefore, it involved a lot of sacrificial rituals, and this law carries punishment.

These are commandments whose reason is not obvious, and the inclination of man is to resist them. The nations of the world argue them—like the prohibition of unclean foods such as pork or fish without scales, etc. A lot of blood sacrifices and offering of animals were required. It was spoken by Moses (Deuteronomy 1:1–6) and written by him in a book, as God instructed (Deuteronomy 31:24). They were not good laws; they were laws whereby the people should not live (Ezekiel 20:25). It made nothing perfect (Hebrews 7:19). It became abolished by the death of Christ on the cross (Ephesians 2:15). He removed the laws that were against us nailing it to the cross (Colossians 2:14).

So it is clear to see that only the laws that were against us for our transgressions are removed. We are no longer required to do them, since Jesus became the ultimate sacrifice for our transgressions. However, as Jesus himself walked in fulfilling the commandments of the moral laws, we also are required to do them. Moral laws are absolute principles, defining the criteria of right doing (whether conceived as a divine ordinance or a truth of reason). You do not have to be a part of any religion to keep these laws. For some people, moral laws are synonymous with the commands of a divine being. For others, moral law is a set of universal rules that should apply to everyone.

Regardless of what one may think, if you are a part of any kingdom, there are laws that must be obeyed and upheld. In God's kingdom, these moral commandments, set out in Exodus 20, are exactly what God has given to us for the saving of our souls and to keep order in our lives. These are good laws. Anyone having a good conscience toward God should not have a problem with carrying them out. Furthermore, you cannot choose to accept some parts and reject the others. It has to be all or nothing.

Many people of God struggle with these laws, and it breathes a terrible confusion among us as believers. We believe and agree that we should not make or bow down to worship idols; we should honour our parents; we should not kill, steal, commit adultery, bear false witness; we shouldn't be covetous; we should have no other God beside the one true God; and that we should not swear unto the Lord in vain. Yet when it comes to keeping the holy day unto the Lord, we are unsure whether we should or shouldn't. In hypocrisy, we pretend not to know what day the Sabbath day is, when God clearly said it is the seventh day.

It seems as if we should revisit our calendars to determine what the first and the last day of the week is. We have already agreed that there are seven days in one week. Now we just need to agree what the first day is. According to our calendar, Sunday is the first day, and Saturday is the seventh. This being the case, we can conclude that we have somehow chosen to be in rebellion or disobedience to what the Lord requires of us.

We cannot choose our own day as a Sabbath unto the Lord, as most have designed to do. God, who created all seven days, has given us six in which we can do that which is for our own well-being. Only on the seventh he has asked us to honour him. Consider then that you must somehow be robbing God of what he has set aside for himself. Do some homework, and see what you come up with.

Oil in Your Lamp

"A little more oil in my lamp, keep it burning; a little more oil in my lamp I pray. A little more oil in my lamp, keep it burning; keep it burning till the break of day." Do you remember those prayerful songs of Zion we used to sing, and how it seemed to have meant something to keep the oil in our lamps burning? But the zeal for the Word of the Lord seems to have worn off, and we are once again left with empty lamps.

In Exodus 27:20, the Lord gave a command to the children of Israel that they use the pure olive oil beaten for the light, to keep the lamp burning always. I believe *burning always* is the important factor in this command. *Periodically* is most certainly unacceptable to God; that is why he made himself so abundantly clear. Although in that dispensation it was the literal lamp with oil of which he spoke, it was very symbolic, back then and now, in reminding us that we are of the light and not the dark.

"Then spoke Jesus again unto them saying, 'I am the light of the world: he who follows me will not walk in darkness, but will have the light of life'" (John 8:12). Here Jesus spoke of the darkness of sin. A child of God without oil is one without light, and that is the same as saying you are without Jesus. "If a man walk in the night, he stumbles, because there is no light in him" (John 11:10).

It is impossible for one to find his way in darkness. Many people are walking around today in the darkness of sin. They are left unprotected from the monsters in the dark and the traps they are unable to see. This should never be in the life of one who claims to know the Lord.

The Word of God must always be burning in our hearts. Psalm 119:11 says, "thy word have I hid in my heart, that I might not sin against thee." Does this mean you will never in your lifetime sin? No, that would be contradictory to God's own Word, which says, "all have sinned and come short of God's Glory." However, keeping our lamps burning will cause us to be more conscious of the sinful nature that lurks within our hearts. Jeremiah 17:9 enlightens us of the deceitfulness of the heart. It is deceitful above all things and desperately wicked.

We need the Word of God burning in our hearts. The entrance of God's Word gives light; it gives understanding unto the simple (Psalm 119:130). There is absolutely no way that the Word of God can enter our hearts without effecting change, no matter who we are. Without the Word of God, we cannot find our way in this world, which is why again in Psalm 119:105, it says, "thy word is a lamp unto my feet and a light unto my path." Direction is uncertain without light, and it causes disaster.

Many years ago, there was a great power outage in our country. Many cities were without light. The stoplights were not functioning, and that created a great disaster for traffic. It was chaos; everywhere people were left in a state of panic and uncertainty. Imagine how it is spiritually when we are without light. There is no difference in what we experience in the natural.

As God's children, we cannot risk our oil running low, not to mention empty. Any honest mechanic will tell you that to maintain your vehicle in proper working order, you must change your oil frequently, as it gets dirty from the pollution in the atmosphere. You must avoid driving on a nearly empty gas tank, as you are also running the risk of damaging the engine and ultimately ending up with a fat mechanic bill. Nearly empty is the same thing as empty; either you are not getting very far or you are not going at all. Either way, it will cost you something.

Let us not be like the five foolish virgins, but like the five wise ones spoken of in Matthew 25. Let us always be filled up and always be prepared. You never know the reason why you may need to use it. Your oil is symbolic of who you are; do not let anyone change that. Protect your oil from foolish people who seek to empty your oil instead of getting their own.

> Afterward came also the other virgins, saying, "Lord, Lord open to us." But he answered and said, "Verily I say unto you, I know you not."
> —Matthew 25:11–12

Chapter 4

Seeking God

Moses said, "I will now turn aside and see this great sight why the bush is not burnt," and when the Lord saw that he turned aside to see, God called to him out of the midst of the bush, and said, "Moses, Moses," and he said "Here Am I" (Exodus 3:3–4). I wonder what God would have done if Moses had ignored this great sight; he was watching Moses to see how he reacted to something mysterious.

God certainly has a way of getting our attention. How many times throughout our lifetime have we had mysterious happenings and chalked it up to nothing? We quickly dismiss the possibility of God trying to get our attention, because we are under the false impression that if the signs don't match up with biblical documentation, such as burning bushes, bright lights, and parting seas, then it could never be God.

God is a God of signs and wonders still today, and he uses modern-day methods to reach us. We just choose to ignore him because we want to do our own thing. How many times do we hear preachers tell us that God wants to use us, and we agree to say yes to his will and way? Yet when the moment of truth comes, we get a sudden change of heart. Ask yourself: what has gotten my attention so tied up that when God is trying to get it, he can't? Is it that you don't believe losing your house, car, husband, wife, children, money, jobs, and many more things that we hold so dear are God's way of getting through to us? Sometimes people and things can become idols in our lives, leaving us with no room at all to seek the true and living God.

God is not the type to thrust anything upon anyone. He wants to see our interest in getting to know him before he can truly work with us. He watches us to see our reaction to his actions. When things begin to get strange around us, it's time to turn aside and seek God; he's waiting. There is no other way to find out our true purpose in life than to seek God's face. I believe Moses was searching for God in his heart; for that reason, the mysterious burning bush piqued his curiosity.

Like Moses, we too should be attracted to the mysterious. God is a God of mystery, and only he can solve them, so observe your surroundings more. Matthew 6:33 says, "seek ye first the kingdom of God, and his righteousness and all other things shall be added unto you." But we don't want to seek; it's too much work. We prefer to put our time into working for the world, to get the things they have to offer but not what God has for us. Take time to seek out God's purpose for your life.

His Countenance

There is something to be said about the countenance of a person who spends time in God's presence. In Exodus 34:29–30, it says, "and it came to pass, when Moses came down from Mount Sinai with the two tablets of testimony in his hands that Moses did not know that the skin of his face shone while he talked with him. And when Aaron and the children of Israel saw Moses, behold, the skin of his face shone; and they were afraid to come near him."

Imagine what an overwhelming sight that must have been for the people beholding him. It certainly did not cause Moses any pain, physical or otherwise, because it said he did not realize. When you are really in the presence of the Lord, your physical appearance is not your major concern. Moses went to get something from the Lord, which he did, and he received more than he imagined. This is who the Lord really is. Whatever you go into his presence for, whether you go to ask him for something or just to worship him, you will always come out with more than you expected.

We may or may not walk away from the Lord's presence with shining faces, but the joy and peace you'll have inside will most definitely be emanating from you, causing people to see you differently. You cannot remain the same if you're truly spending time in the presence of the Lord. In Psalm 16:11, King David, from his own experiences being in the Lord's presence, declared that there are pleasures and fullness of joy. Partial joy just will not do. God doesn't do partial anything. You cannot overcome much with just partial joy; it's like driving someplace far away on just half a tank of gas without funds to buy more. It just won't work; you'll never reach it. Neither will you get far in your spiritual journey with partial joy.

A child of God without joy is a defeated one. In Matthew 7:16, Jesus said, "You shall know them by their fruits." God's children should be some of the most beautiful people in the world, not vain beauty but a beauty that will not fade away through trials and tribulations. Nehemiah 8:10 tells us, "The joy of the Lord is your strength." A happy and cheerful child of God is one who is without doubt, spending time in the Lord's presence. I have proved it. No one is ever able to tell whether or not I have trouble in my life, but I do, just like other people; but spending time with the Lord gives me a peace inside that surpasses these challenges, as God promised.

It really saddens me to say that some of the most miserable countenances are worn by people who profess to know God. It's not that you are not entitled to your emotions, but if you are going to represent Christ, you should at least be able to put them under subjection to face those with whom you will come in contact.

I have noticed that after I had spent time in fasting and prayer, talking with the Lord, people would comment on my countenance, how beautiful and young I looked. It is not a look that can be obtained from expensive top-of-the-line facial products. I have seen many people nicely dressed up with beautiful faces and sad countenances. There is no makeup that can turn your frown upside down; only the peace of God abiding inside can do that. The Lord told Moses to bless the children of Israel in Numbers 6:24–26, saying, "the Lord bless you and keep you, the Lord make his face to shine upon you, lift up his countenance upon you and give you peace."

If the Lord's countenance is not on your face, what countenance are you showing? One day, while I was in the grocery store, I noticed a lady who was showing an angry countenance. In an attempt to make her smile, I simply said, "Smile. It's not that bad." She smiled a half smile and said, "I am so stressed." I don't think she realized that stress was ruining her countenance. This encounter caused me to pay closer attention to my countenance.

If you do not spend time in God's presence, stress will move in on your countenance and smear you with wrinkles and lines. I have heard many older people who live for the Lord testify that joy in the Lord is what keeps them looking so beautiful. This also is God's promise to beautify the meek with salvation. Try it for yourself.

Time with God

Moses went up into the clouds and got up into the mount, and Moses was in the mountain forty days and forty nights (Exodus 24:18). As I look into this passage, I think, *What dedication!* Or is it that we think Moses didn't have anything better to do with his time? I am pretty sure he could be busy doing otherwise, just as we do, yet he chose to do what God would have him do. God is still calling us today to the metaphoric mountain, where he is able to communicate and reveal some things to us; but in our fast-paced environment, some of us cannot find forty hours, forty minutes, *forty seconds,* let alone forty days.

We spend moments in between our busy schedule speculating about God, instead of really getting to know him up close and personally. Just as we judge each other, we judge the Almighty God, our Creator. God could never do this or that. He is not that kind of God. For this very reason, the Lord said that his people perish for lack of knowledge. It is unrealistic to presume that you know anyone without spending time with them. Furthermore, you should have no expectation of anyone you are not fairly acquainted with.

Moses would not have received the laws of God without spending that quality time with him. God expects that same quality time from us. Think of being in a relationship and never having any time for each other. It would lead one to doubt your loyalty or sincerity toward the relationship.

You need to develop a love connection with God, so you can build trust in him. Solid relationships are based upon trust. When you have this trust, you will be more confident that the one you are in a relationship with will remain faithful to you and watch your back.

I believe most marital problems in the beginning stages of marriage happen because the couple are still getting to know each other. It is hard to trust a stranger. You may call me a sceptic. I just don't believe in love at first sight. Fascination, yes. For human beings, it takes time to develop that real, deep love for each other. Notice I said *real.*

We use the word *love* very loosely. We love our car, clothes, pets, food, jewellery, etc., and we throw people into the mix. Just as we discard the things we no longer "love," this is the very way we treat people. This is not so with God; he loves us in spite of our falling short in his expectations of us. While we were yet sinners, God gave his only Son to take our place in death caused by sin—our sin.

How many of us are willing to die for someone we love, regardless of their fairly deserved penalty? At the first sign of trouble, we are ready to bail, convinced that the person just wasn't right or easy to love. When we find the right person, we decide, things will be much better. Hogwash. I can admit I am guilty as charged; can you? You would be surprised how many churchgoers claim to have a relationship with God, but at the first sign of trouble, they turn to someone or something else for help.

If you have an opportunity to talk with couples who have been in long-lasting marriages, they will tell you they are now reaping the rewards of working on their marriage. Now they can finally enjoy the fruits of their labour. Some who did not stay will tell you they wish they had stayed. Now they realize the grass is not greener on the other side. Relationships are hard work. Anything worthwhile you are building takes time and dedication. You just have to be willing to see it through. Just think of how rewarding it must be, spending time with God.

I don't know about you, but I find spending time with God is much more rewarding than spending time with people. When you really think about it, people deplete you. So much is expected of us from people everywhere—people we know and don't know. We give out so much at home, church, and school; bill collectors and tax collectors are knocking on our doors and calling our telephones. It never ends. We are so exhausted through it all, there is very little time left for God.

When we begin to see God as our source, our focus and priorities will change. You need not to do anything other than sit quietly in his presence and let him pour into you what people cannot. Let him shower you with mercy, grace, love, joy, peace, and most of all revelation of who he is. Unless you spend time with God, you will have nothing to give others.

When I don't get to spend quality time with him, I am unequipped to cope with the pressures of life imposed upon me by others. I love people and love to help those I see in need; however, not spending time with God can defeat the whole purpose. We can cause harm to others, rather than doing good, simply because our priorities are in the wrong place. Spend some time with God, and he will make you into a blessing to others around you.

> Blessed are they that keep his testimonies,
> and that seek him with the whole heart.
> —Psalm 119:2

Chapter 5

Don't Look Back

"*I*s not this the word that we did tell thee in Egypt, saying, let us alone that we may serve the Egyptians? For it had been better for us to serve the Egyptians, than that we should die in the wilderness" (Exodus 14:12). How sad is that statement? It is still being made by many professing to be believers. The first sign of trouble on their journey with the Lord, and they are ready to give up their salvation they cried for, to go back to being prisoners of sin.

I know that being oppressed can affect your state of mind, but snap out of it! Never once did God promise that it would be an easy journey. You just need to believe he would not take you this far only to leave you. Hebrews 13:5–6 says, "let your conversation be without covetousness and be content with such things as ye have; for he have said, I will never leave thee nor forsake thee. So that we may boldly say, the Lord is my helper, and I will not fear what man shall do unto me."

It is with a made-up mind that you must follow Christ; otherwise, you will keep looking back at the things you've left behind as something better, another deception of the enemy. Although Paul the apostle knew what it was to live life with all the trimmings, so to speak, he stumbled upon some of the most outrageous difficulties when he was called into the ministry.

Nevertheless, he could still say in Philippians 3:13–14, "forgetting those things which are behind and reaching forth unto those things which are before, I press toward the mark for the prize of the high calling of God in Christ Jesus."

Paul was looking forward to the prize that was before him, because by faith, he believed that what he had left behind was nothing in comparison to God's promise. God promised to lead the children of Israel into a place that was better. The problem is, they expected it to be done through the pharaoh's fly-by-night magic. "Poof, and it's done!;" But God doesn't work magic, he performs miracles, and in those miracles, he likes to get us involved. He makes it so we will appreciate what we get when we get it.

Stop being so covetous; it's a sin that gets you into situations that separate you from God. In Philippians 4:11–12, Paul said he had learned to be content in whatsoever state he found himself in, how to abase and to abound, everywhere in all things. He was instructed both to be hungry, both to abound and to suffer need, and so must we also as followers of Christ. "I had rather be a door keeper in the house of my God, than to dwell in the tent of wickedness" (Psalm 84:10).

People today are just looking for quick fixes. Their needs are not being met by God quickly enough. It's this kind of behaviour that always gets us in trouble. Some people would rather sell their souls to the devil than wait on God. They say miracles take too long, so they choose to put their trust in magic.

Trust in the Lord

"Then Pharaoh also called the wise men and the sorcerers: Now the magicians of Egypt they also did in like manner with their enchantments. For they cast down every man his rod, and they became serpents; but Aaron's rod swallowed up their rods" (Exodus 7:11–12). Many church-goers turn away from God in their hearts, seeking the help of magicians, sorcerers, and enchanters, because they are able to do a few tricks, resembling God's handiwork. The key word here is *resembling*. You should know that you are putting your trust in something that will obviously be destroyed and is only temporary.

In this passage, God's serpent swallowed up those of the magicians, and that should be an eye-opener for you. Don't be blinded by the lies of tricksters. Open your eyes to the truth. Man is exactly that: "man," made by God, and we must learn to respect the power of our Creator. If you are daring enough to challenge God's strength, then I have the confidence to tell you that you will lose every time. God never backs down from a challenge; he welcomes it. In fact, he laughs at that kind of misplaced ambition. "He that sit in the heavens shall laugh; the Lord shall have them in derision" (Psalm 2:4). It is foolish to trust in man's help over God's. The same breath in you is the same as in the magicians, which, at any given time, God can take away as he pleases.

To turn away from your Creator and turn to man for help is evil, and there is nothing rewarding in that. Isaiah 30:1–3 says, "Woe to the rebellious children, said the Lord, that take counsel; but not of me and that cover with a covering, but not of my spirit that they may add sin to sin, that walk to go down into Egypt and have not asked of my mouth; to trust in the strength of Pharaoh and to trust in the shadow of Egypt! Therefore shall the strength of Pharaoh be your shame; and the trust in the shadow of Egypt, your confusion." God is clearly telling you that putting your trust in the deceptions of man will only bring shame and confusion to your life. The reason God gave his people such a strong warning about seeking help from the Egyptians is because of their beliefs in idolatry. They did not trust in the one true God; they could only lead according to their customs.

People who turn away from God or simply do not trust him can all be traced back to fear. As the saying goes, "we fear what we don't understand." The lack of understanding is because of our lack of knowledge. Many times, we are afraid without knowing why; it is a learned behaviour. Fear is environmental; we feed off each other's fear, whether we realize it or not.

I know someone who is afraid of spiders and will not go near them. One day, as I watched this person frantically running from a spider, I pointed out to her that she had the power over the spider, considering the spider was already at her mercy, fearing being squished at any time. I gave her something to think about. The only reason why we fear is because we have not been taught what to embrace and what not to. Therefore, our natural reaction is to react the way we have seen others react, especially people we love and trust.

Once I was vacationing in Jamaica, and my friend was kind enough to accommodate me. While I was in my room, I noticed a lizard crawling on the wall. I didn't run away frantically, but I was frantic nonetheless. I refused to fall asleep and stayed up all night, making sure I knew of the lizard's whereabouts at all times. In the morning, I reported the incident to my friend and her husband, and they were respectfully astounded at my fear of this small reptile, considering they live with them as pets. The reason I reacted this way is because my grandmother was terrified of them. I learned her behaviour; therefore, her fear became my fear.

We all have something we are afraid of, whether we are able to see it or not. Fearing what we can see is different from fearing what we cannot see. While we may be able to discard, damage or destroy what we can see, it is impossible to physically destroy what we cannot see. This is considered spiritual, and people are more afraid or threatened by spiritual things than natural things, since oftentimes spiritual things carry a more powerful presence. I believe nothing can harm us of the spiritual, as long as we are under God's protection.

Anything of the spiritual realm is really powerless in this realm without a body of some sort to use as a host. This is the art of witchcraft, the ability to invoke spirits into any living or dead thing, so as to manipulate, control or direct them, in order to frighten you to harm or death. For instance, if a person who's been dead and buried appears to you, your reaction depends on your beliefs or state of mind. If you see this as nothing but evil and unnatural, you may faint. You may even be afraid to the point of a heart attack if your heart is weak. On the other hand, if you believe that it's all right for your dead mother to be standing before you while her body is in the grave, you may have no problem having her taking up residence in your home and conversing and interacting with her.

If your reaction matches either of the two examples, you are clearly in bondage to lack of knowledge or fear. First of all, the only thing that God has to do with the dead is to bring them back to life; he is a God of the living. These miracles are done for the purpose of glorifying God, not to deceive us. Another thing God will do is prepare our hearts for such an encounter. God knows that our minds are filled with fear, so he allows a spirit of comfort to tell us "Fear not." So if we are not being comforted, we are encountering an evil source. If we are at a place spiritually to stand up to such a force and command it to go, it has to leave. If not, it will stay to accomplish its mission for which it was sent. This means you do not have any spiritual authority, and this is not good.

If you are the type of person who acts like the welcoming committee for these trespassers—which is what they are—then you may as well be a worker of witchcraft. Only these types of people play with the dead. Yes, it is called playing with the dead. If you are not resurrecting them, the only thing you should be doing to them is showing them to the door, the way back to wherever they came from. You should never be comfortable with any other spirit around you except for the holy presence of God. As long as the spirit of God is within you, no other spirit can abide except for the angels of God protecting you.

Because there are good and evil spirits in the atmosphere, which we aren't able to see with our natural eyes, we need the spirit of God to be able to discern them. Sometimes these spirits can be felt or heard, and if they are from the dark side, they will make you feel uncomfortable if you are of the light. Both light and darkness carry a presence, a very strong presence, so if you do not have the Holy Spirit to discern the difference, you will be afraid of both. This is why God tells us "fear not." Fear is of the devil. If we find we are afraid of spirits, whether they are manifesting in body or not, we must examine ourselves to see if we truly have Christ within. We must ask ourselves, are we good or evil? "The righteous are bold as a lion" (Proverbs 28:1).

Many people, instead of reaching out for God's help, resort to seeking help from the very people who are only able to invoke evil spirits. They will suggest everything for protection against these spirits except for prayer and trust in God. People can only give you the help they know. Any help that comes from any earthly thing is susceptible to destruction and therefore can only be a temporary solution. By now, we should all know that.

Honestly, it's as if we have made no progress at all. We keep saying how we have evolved, how we have increased in knowledge, but it seems to me as though the more things change, the more they stay the same. It is shocking to see how primitive we still are. As far as I am concerned, any type of magic, whether it's witchcraft, sorcery, necromancy, obeah, or what have you, is primitive thinking and behaviour. These are all the things people would do when trying to find a solution to their problems when they did not know God. The fear of darkness was upon the earth, and it caused people to do foolish things that were not edifying or uplifting to their souls.

Now that the light has shined into the darkness and we have seen and learned so much, it truly is abominable that we would revert back to such primitive practices. Many people would rather spend thousands of dollars for a sorcerer to help them solve their problems than to turn to God who made them. Some people will spend their last dime thinking that the solution to their problems is in the reading of their palms or the reading of some cards or simply drinking some brew or killing an animal.

After going to any source of witchcraft, your troubles have only just begun. Seeking protection from them is the same as seeking protection from Satan, since he is their source. If you are still afraid all the time after receiving their so-called help, then you have not been helped. The whole idea of protection is that you feel safe and secure; you are confident in the one that is protecting you. Think about it. Don't you feel taken after spending a thousand dollars for a beaded bracelet or some other foolish thing for your so-called guard? Can't you see that it is not the bracelet protecting you but your belief? This being the case, can you not will yourself to believe in God as your protector? Yes! You can; try it!

Do not allow yourself to be controlled by your surroundings. Our minds are the most powerful weapons against anything, so do not limit yourself to earthly things. Think outside the box that only contains your five senses. Soar above them; you do not have to touch, taste or handle something to believe it. Acquaint yourself with your spiritual self; it is far more powerful than your natural self. Your flesh is afraid, not your spirit.

Before I got saved, I was afraid all the time. Just being alone made me afraid. At certain times of the night, when the darkness was very thick, I felt as though I was surrounded by demons. I was terrified to sleep in my own home. After a while, I learned that someone who was heavy into witchcraft was trying to control me with it. I had no understanding of what was happening to me until God spoke to me and told me not to be afraid. I should trust him to protect me. After hearing God's voice and believing him, I was no longer afraid, and I'm not afraid to this day. You would be a fool to turn to witchcraft workers for help. Their only delight is sending you on a fool's errand, which they take great delight in doing.

The more afraid they make you, the more they will be able to control you; the more they control you, the more they will benefit from you. Don't tell me how intelligent you are and then pay a man to protect you from evil or to make your lover stay put or to keep your job or to have lots of money. What if he dies? What would you do, find another one? You need to learn to trust and rely on God; that was my only deliverance, and it can be for you too, if you just believe it. Instead of someone making you afraid, they will be afraid of you.

After I was no longer afraid, my enemies began spreading rumours of my being a witchcraft worker. So I learned that when people aren't able to control you by such means, they automatically assume that your help is coming from the same source. They are so far removed from God that they do not consider the possibility of his being able to deliver us from evil. When the perfect love of God came into my heart, fear had to go, just as when the light came in, darkness had to go. If you are to be a fool for anyone, let it be for God.

There is no power greater than the almighty God, and you need to believe in that. Take God at his word; he is no trickster. Meditate on Psalms 121 and 125. If you can put so much confidence in man, how much more should you put in his maker? "It is better to trust in the Lord than to put confidence in man" (Psalm 118:8). I want to encourage you with a song written by Tony C., sung by Whitney Houston: "Love will save the day." They are actually words to live by. Who or what is love but God?

God's Grace

There is an old phrase that says you can take the people out of the country, but you can't take the country out of the people. This is true for some believers. Although God has called us out of a life of sin to partake in his righteousness, we continue to indulge in our sinful ways. How many times do we ask God for grace, yet when we receive it, we regress right back to our old selves? It's time for us to pull up our socks and get serious with God. What shall we say then? Shall we continue to sin, that grace may abound? God forbid. "How shall we that are dead to sin, live any longer therein?" (Romans 6:1–2).

Grace should be treated with appreciation and respect. Galatians 6:7 warns us, "be not deceived, God is not mocked: for whatsoever a man sows, that shall he reap." We have far too long played around with God's grace. We take for granted his character trait of longsuffering. Ecclesiastes 8:11 explains our ongoing wickedness. "Because sentence against an evil work is not executed speedily, therefore the heart of the sons of man is fully set in them to do evil."

Many believe that God's delayed reaction is their licence to continue in their evil works. Some say he can't be real; others say he's dead. I assure you, he's very much real and alive, and his timely way of conduct is what I have come to love the most about his character. He knows that man is prone to sin, and therefore he is justified, in that he has given us ample time for repentance. Second Chronicles 7:14 pleads with us, "If my people, which are called by my name, shall humble themselves, and pray, and seek my face, and turn from their wicked ways, then will I hear from heaven, and will forgive their sin, and heal their land."

Hear God's plea for repentance today and surrender. Let's not be too busy being people who are only Christ like, but people who are living according to the Word. God requires us to demonstrate the principles of his kingdom, and to do that, we must know what those principles are. Our thoughts, speech and actions should be a reflection of who he is.

Let not sin therefore reign in your mortal body,
that you should obey it in the lusts thereof.
Neither yield your members as
instruments of unrighteousness unto sin:
but yield yourselves unto God, as those
that are alive from the dead, and your
members as instruments of righteousness
unto God.
—Romans 6:12–13

Chapter 6

Witches, Wizards, Sorcerers

$\mathcal{S}$ome people still aren't convinced that witches, wizards and sorcerers really do exist. To them, there is no such thing; it is only a myth. But the Word of God says they do, and that is all the convincing I personally need. Who or what are they exactly? They are individuals who are engaged in the works of witchcraft, also known as witchery, which is the practice of magic, especially black magic, the use of spells and the invocation of spirits. They are said to have direct communication with Satan. Witches, wizards, sorcerers, diviners and necromancers are all similarly linked to such practices.

The word *witchcraft* has been derived from the word *Wicca*, which means "the wise one." The concept and practice of witchcraft can be traced to the early days of mankind's existence and is considered a pagan worship or religion. All their works are dark and evil, which is diametrically opposed to the principles of God's kingdom, which is of pure goodness and light.

Although some are still sceptical of their existence, they are quite often talked about in children's storybooks and movies. They are depicted as the villains who oppress the lives of people with good hearts and the potential to vanquish their evil works. The people will therefore not tolerate them. From an early age, our children are taught about them, and why shouldn't they be?

The Lord would not have us to be ignorant of Satan's devices, says 2 Corinthians 2:11.

In the story of Cinderella, her wicked stepmother saw the potential of her beautiful heart, and tried everything to crush her. Snow White was put into a deep sleep from which she should not awaken by a poisonous apple she received from her wicked stepmother who disguised herself as a pitiful old lady. Rapunzel was locked in a tower by a witch to keep her from her true love.

You may think these stories are written as entertainment for our children. These stories are written as truth hidden behind a myth, which leaves you to come to your own conclusion. It's much like the television show *Ripley's Believe It or Not*. The stories are almost beyond our human comprehension, and yet they are quite often the truth. The lesson these stories have commonly taught us, in spite of their exaggeration for our entertainment, is that evil does exist. Whether we choose to label them or not does not change the fact that evil is real. Another thing we cannot change is this: whatever God says you are, that is what you are. It cannot be altered by man, regardless of our disagreement and disapproval.

One thing these stories all have in common is that the good characters always come out the hero or heroine because evil can never prevail over good. This can be compared with the love of Jesus Christ, which protects us from these forces of darkness. We make ourselves comfortable calling them fairytales because we are too afraid to deal with them.

The thing about locking everything you can't deal with away in a closet is that one day, when you go in to put away something else, it could all tumble down on you, making your life harder than if you had just dealt with it at first. That's how you have to deal with witches—at first. That's why God says in Exodus 22, "Do not allow them." Do not allow them to influence your life in any way, to do what they do.

These forces of darkness plague and terrorize our lives every day in secret and need to be addressed in our prayers to God. Church, we are not doing our jobs. We ourselves have dismissed the reality of them, leaving us without borders for them to create havoc in our lives. In 1 Kings 20–21, you can find the story of Jezebel, whom the Bible clearly pointed out as one who practiced witchcraft by way of incantations and spells, otherwise known as word curse.

We have been programmed to believe that witchcraft is all about mixing brews and casting spells, but it is much deeper than you know. There is no hex, vex, spell or curse that can be carried out or activated without words. Life and death are in the power of the tongue, according to Proverbs 18:21. Jezebel sent out a curse to Elijah, which carried a spirit of fear, saying, "So let the gods do to me, and more also if I make not thy life as the life of one of them by tomorrow about this time" (1 Kings 19:2).

It is often questioned why Elijah, who had such powerful anointing, would run for his life at the words of Jezebel—a woman no less, some would say—as if evil is less impacting through a woman. It is easy for us to say what we would and would not do when we ourselves aren't wearing the shoes. Anyone who understands what witchcraft is all about would know that the only thing more powerful than witchcraft is the love of God.

Witchcraft is all about fear. The power of fear is used by witchcraft workers to control, manipulate and deceive their victims. Whenever you're feeling afraid, especially as a child of God, you know that something is not right. Fear is not of God; it is Satan's device. When Adam and Eve were caused to sin through his deception, the first spirit that entered into them was fear. They became fearful of the very God who created them, something they had never experienced before, which proves that when we aren't feeling close to God, we can fall prey to Satan's devices.

So what does this say about Elijah? What I can tell you from experience is that because we have the sin nature of Adam and

Eve, no matter how anointed we are, there are days when we will not feel close to God, whether or not we have committed sin. That's when any dark spirits will try to overpower us. Elijah was feeling very alone and depressed, thinking he was the only prophet left of all who were killed, so it was easy for such a spirit to influence his thinking.

This spirit is deadly because its sole purpose is to disconnect you from God. As long as you are afraid, it is hard for you to trust God. Not trusting in God makes you feel powerless, and as long as you feel powerless, you cannot overcome fear. Jezebel knew all about the power of fear. In fact, all witchcraft workers know about the power of fear. It is their greatest weapon.

King Saul, on the other hand, put a different spin on witchcraft when he outwardly disobeyed God by sparing the life of Agag, the king of the Amalekites, and then insulting him by making a sacrifice with what he had taken from them. Samuel informed Saul that rebellion is as the sin of witchcraft (1 Samuel 15:23). As you can see, disobedience to God is also considered witchcraft. In fact, all works of evil, whether done in deed or word, are a result of our disobedience to God. Disobedience is the mother of sin, which opened the gateway for the forces of evil to destroy us.

God is totally against anything that is aimed to put his people in bondage. In Deuteronomy 18:10–15, the Lord gave specific instructions to his people not to let anyone of such kind be found among them. He told them that anyone who is using divination, an observer of times, an enchanter, a witch, a charmer, a consulter with familiar spirits, a wizard or necromancer is an abomination unto him. Whatever they needed to know, he would raise up a prophet from their brethren to tell them all he commanded.

Let me emphasize the word *need*, because too many times, we get ourselves in trouble just by being inquisitive in things that don't concern us. This is when we become impatient and careless. If God isn't responding to our calls or if we feel our needs are not being met by him, the temptation to turn to such sources becomes great. This is what happened to King Saul. When he could no longer hear from God, he sought after a woman who had a familiar spirit to conjure up the dead prophet Samuel, to tell him what God had to say (1 Samuel 28). Clearly, he was out of his mind!

God is a specialist in our needs, and therefore, we should wait on him to provide or tell us whatever we need to know. Even though this is what he promised to do by raising up a prophet, we don't trust God to tell us anything. "His ways of doing things do not work for us; he's too slow." Well, I have news for you! With my own eyes, I witnessed people who have lost their minds when they messed with witchcraft.

Anything outside of God's power is temporary, I assure you. Therefore, it is not effective in fixing any of your problems permanently. It's similar to crack cocaine; it gives you a temporary high, and then it drops you like a ton of bricks. If you don't get out of it right away, it will destroy your whole life.

Modern-day witchcraft is in full effect. You would be surprised to know who relies on it for their bread and butter. Everyone wants a quick fix so they can forget their suffering. Jesus Christ must bear the cross while everyone goes free. I will not sit comfortably and complacently as the church does when it concerns this act of rebellion that has so obviously manifested among us. It's time for action.

We need to get back to Christ like, spirit-filled lives. We must equip ourselves to combat the works of the flesh that are fast leading us into destruction. Galatians 5:19–21 points out the works of the flesh that are manifest: adultery, fornication, uncleanness, lasciviousness, Idolatry, witchcraft, hatred, variance, emulations, wrath, strife, seditions, heresies, envy, murder, drunkenness, revelries, and such like. As I have told you before they who do such things shall not inherit the kingdom of God. This is the Word of God.

Although we are no longer burning witchcraft workers at the stake, they can indeed be burned with the fire of the Holy Spirit. The fire of God burns up such wickedness. Salvation is for them who so choose to turn away from their evil ways. No real child of God should embrace a person who practices witchcraft as a friend; they are enemies of God. They are deceptive, manipulating and controlling. They leave nothing to faith. Their whole motive is to bend or alter the minds of those who they seek to control.

I have had my own personal encounters with those who would destroy my life had it not been for God. This is why I can tell you there is no power greater than Almighty God. So don't be tricked or fooled into thinking they are able to help you. Let me just add that witchery is not limited to gender. Often, the term *witch* is associated with women. Men are known as *wizards* or *sorcerers*. Whether it is witchery, sorcery or wizardry, they are all known as black magic. Acts 8:9 tells of a man called Simon who used sorcery to bewitch the people of Samaria. He declared himself to be someone great and the people exalted him in such a manner.

As great as Simon thought himself to be, when he saw the power of God moving upon his manservant Peter, he coveted it. Thinking that the power of God is for sale, Simon wanted to buy it for himself. Today, there are many "Simons" among us in the church, aren't there? Those greedy, small people who think that their money can buy them power. If you have to buy power, then you're not of God.

God's church is not led by magic. It is led by the Spirit of the Lord. Many leaders of God's people, who just covet the position and the power of the anointing, ultimately turn into magicians. These charlatans throw down their proverbial rods to make it look as if they are the real deal. I urge you to turn away from such false leaders today, before you are destroyed by God's greater power.

Don't be fooled, people. You should know the difference between *magic* and *the anointing*. God's power is not used to control or manipulate the minds of people. Where the spirit of the Lord is, there is liberty. You should never feel as though you are in bondage, oppressed or controlled under any leadership. Let's not just get with the program, let's make sure that all that is being done is in conjunction with God's Word. Many people of God are not even aware that they are held in bondage by the works of witchcraft! We are sometimes so deceived by magic that we cannot tell the difference between *clean* and *unclean*.

It is hurtful to watch as people are hoodwinked into believing something that is designed to keep them powerless. So wake up! Wake up! And begin to pray against this evil that fight against the church of God. You may not realize how much power you have as a child of God, but his power is real, his power is yours and you need to use it. Trust in God's power, not false power. "For God hath not given us the spirit of fear; but of power, and of love, and of a sound mind" (2 Timothy 1:7).

Crossing Over

"Fear and Dread shall fall upon them; by the greatness of thy arm they shall be still as stone till thy people pass over, O Lord, till thy people pass over, which thou has purchased" (Exodus 15:16).

The enemy is still in pursuit of God's people, and they will never stop until God stops them. They are always pursuing, and God is always delivering.

Now more than ever, we seem to be battling the forces of evil that are trying to stop us from serving our God. Until they have this experience of fear and dread falling upon them, they will never be able to escape. Persistence can be a good thing unless it's done vindictively and maliciously. There are still metaphorical Egyptians to escape from and metaphorical Red Seas to cross. They just refuse to let you cross over to your destiny. Your life is a constant struggle because they insist on oppressing you.

The moment it appears to those Egyptians that you are escaping, they come to escort you back to the place of oppression. Know that when you feel that your back is up against the wall, that's the time the Lord will show you his mighty hand. Fear and dread does not come upon these people without the divine intervention of Almighty God. They neither regard him nor his people, but in spite of their utter disregard, they will and must acknowledge his power.

In Deuteronomy 2:25, the Lord told Moses, "This day will I begin to put the fear of thee and the dread of thee upon the nations that are under the whole heaven, who shall hear report of thee, and shall tremble, and be in anguish because of thee." We need this same fear and dread to fall upon those who continue to oppress us.

Many of God's people who have the potential to achieve greatness are suffering through this oppression. Nevertheless, be encouraged! There is a day of salvation. If you don't believe me, believe God's Word. In Exodus 14:13, Moses told the people of God, "Fear not, stand still and see the salvation of the Lord. Which he will show you today: For the Egyptians whom you see today, you shall see them again no more forever."

Trust the Lord to make a way of escape for you. First Corinthians 10:13 offers reassurance. "There hath no temptation taken you; but such as is common to man: but God is faithful, who will not suffer you to be tempted above that ye are able, but with the temptation also make a way to escape that he may be able to bear it."

Whatever enemy or Red Sea is trying to stop you, just stand still and watch the Lord make a way of escape for you. He will never leave you in the hands of the enemy. You will cross over to your place of purpose and promise.

Whenever you are feeling as if all is lost, and there is no way your dreams or visions will come true remember that God is able to finish whatever he starts. No matter what the hindrances are, or how high the obstacles may seem, there is no challenge too great for God.

There is a song I learned long ago written by (**Gloria Griffin)** titled; "God Specializes" that goes like this:

> "Is there any river that seems to be uncrossable?
> Is there any mountain you cannot tunnel through?
> God specialises in the things which are impossible
> And he will do what no other power but holy power can do.
> God has, will and always deliver his people."

> I called upon the Lord in distress:
> the Lord answered me,
> and set me in a large place.
> —Psalm 118:5

Chapter 7

Power in Jesus' Name

*F*or far too long, we have taken the name of Jesus for granted. We are still wondering what to do with it. There are great benefits in the name of Jesus Christ, but we won't discover them unless we begin to use it. When God told Moses to go and tell his people that he had been sent him to deliver them, Moses was afraid. Even though God had identified himself as the God of their forefathers, Abraham, Isaac and Israel, Moses feared that it would not be enough. Moses wanted a name to give to the people, but he could not be convinced that "I AM" was enough. To demonstrate his awesome power, God gave Moses a rod that was imbued with divine power.

That rod represented Jesus Christ the Mighty Deliverer, and this same power is available to us in this modern day. We need to learn to use the name of Jesus Christ more, so that unbelievers can truly know that he is real. Just as Moses had to learn to use the rod, we must learn to wield his power. Like Moses and the people, we also have a tendency to stand around, frightened and uncertain. We don't know what to do with the power we possess, so we do nothing. It is time for the people of God to start demonstrating their power!

A very powerful demonstration of the name of Jesus is in Acts 3:6, where Peter the apostle spoke to a man who was lame from birth, saying "silver and gold have I none; but such as I have give I thee, in the name of Jesus Christ of Nazareth rise up and walk."

Whether or not Peter had money is not the issue. He still would not have been able to heal that lame man without the power of the name of Jesus. So it is now. No matter how much money you may have, you cannot use it to save your souls. I'm telling you now: You need Jesus! "Jesus Christ is far above principality, dominion, power, and might and every name that is named, not only in this world, but also in that which is to come" (Ephesians 1:21). I have never read or heard of any other name with that kind of power.

Therefore, as children of the Most High God who have access to that name, we should walk in confidence of what it can do. "That at the name of Jesus, every knee shall bow, of things in heaven and things in earth, and things under the earth and that every tongue should confess that Jesus Christ is Lord to the Glory of God the father" (Philippians 2:10–11).

There is no other method or name by which you can truly receive deliverance from anything that may have you in bondage. "Neither is there salvation in any other, for there is none other name under heaven given among men whereby we must be saved" (Acts 4:12). Use the name of Jesus; it's your victory. In John 14:14, Jesus himself said, "If you shall ask anything in my name, I will do it."

House of Bondage

In Exodus 20:2, God spoke to the children of Israel. "I am the Lord your God, which have brought you out of the Land of Egypt, out of the house of bondage." One thing that is most certain: when God does anything mighty in our lives, he puts his stamp of approval on it. He will not share his glory with man. No one cared about you when you were in bondage, but as soon as the Lord delivers you, someone else is looking to take credit for it. No wonder why some would find themselves right back in their situation until they have learned to give God the glory.

Any sin committed as a result of presumptuousness, ignorance or carelessness automatically puts you in a place of bondage. As children of God, we are prone to such situations, "because your adversary the devil, as a roaring lion, walketh about, seeking whom he may devour" (1 Peter 5:8).

No man can take you out of any house of bondage situation. Zechariah 4:6 explains that is the devil's trap, and cannot be done by our own might or power, only by the spirit of God. If there is one thing that I've learned, it's that the enemies of our soul do not want us to make any kind of progress in our lives as children of God. Therefore, they are always looking for ways to bring us into bondage. He especially seeks out those who have the ability and strength to achieve greatness, and often through our own disobedience, we give him an occasion to accomplish his mission.

The story of Samson is one that tugs at my heartstrings. Unfortunately, though there may be great strength within us, there is also weaknesses the enemy can exploit to bring us into bondage. In Samson's case, his hair was his strength. His compassion was the weakness his enemy chose to exploit. Many believe that compassion is a good quality to possess; I would most certainly agree. However, even a good quality within us, when exercised without wisdom, knowledge and understanding has the ability to land us right back into the house of bondage.

In Judges 14:16, Samson's wife cried before him for seven days. She appealed to that compassion within him, and he gave in. Throughout chapter 16, Delilah appeals to that same compassionate quality landed him in the Philistine's house of bondage. Close the doors of your heart to such the malicious spirits of enticement and manipulation. The Word of God is a discerner; it is helpful to you in counteracting these orchestrations induced by principalities.

If you truly study the Word of God, you will see that our father Abba does not fold under the pressures of our manipulative tears, and neither should we. It's time we wise up to the devil's tactics. As I stated before, in 1 Peter 5:8, we are advised to "Be sober, be vigilant; because your adversary the devil, as a roaring Lion, walketh about seeking, whom he may devour." If you believe that you're in this house of bondage, and you long to be delivered, you must first acknowledge any act of disobedience you have committed to God through prayer. Seek him earnestly from your heart. The one thing God cannot ignore is humility to him. When coupled with our acknowledgement of him being the Almighty God, that is enough to move his hand.

Although God moves through process and time, he also is present in times of trouble he understands to be urgent. Gods' ways are past finding out and don't let anyone tell you differently. When Queen Esther found out the enemy had sent out a decree to annihilate the Jews from which there were no clause to change it, she took action. She prostrated before God for three days, fasting without food or water, and the God of our salvation delivered.

The old dragon is not wiser than the Most-high God. With him, there is always a way even when we don't see it. This same Samson was able to destroy the Philistines by calling out for God's help through prayer. God doesn't just *specialize* in deliverance, he *delights* in it. Do not delay in seeking him for yours today. When he does deliver you, do not forget to first give him the glory.

"There hath no temptation taken you but such as is common to man: but God is faithful, who will not suffer you to be tempted above that you are able; but will with the temptation also make a way to escape, that you may be able to bear it" (1 Corinthians 10:13).

Chapter 8

God Said It

*S*omewhere along this pilgrim journey, we have all wondered if we still believe God. But whatever rough patches we may find ourselves in, that is precisely the time we need to believe in God more. As we learned in Exodus 9:5–6, he is a keeper of his word. "The Lord appointed a set time, saying, Tomorrow the Lord shall do this thing in the land, and the Lord did that thing on the morrow …"

It's clear to me that what when God says he will do something, he means it. If the word goes out of his mouth, it surely will be accomplished. Each time he fulfills his promises to us, the Lord clearly places a distinction between his character and that of humans. We cannot treat God the same way we treat people. "The Lord is not slack concerning his promise, as some men count slackness" (2 Peter 3:9). This means that you can count on him delivering whatever he promised. You can count, however, on people breaking their promises under certain circumstances or deliberation.

My encouragement to you is this: keep your faith in God. If he doesn't give you what he promised on your time, don't start throwing tantrums like some spoiled child. God sometimes will give a direct word for today or tomorrow and sometimes not. Abraham, our forefather of faith, had to wait for many years before receiving the promise of God. He waited in faith, and that's what matters.

Many biblical patriarchs and modern-day men and women of God who trusted in him have been rewarded for their patience and faith. They waited for their promise and they received it as they have testified. Be patient with the Lord; perhaps the promise is delayed for a good reason, but it is never denied. We expect so much from him, yet we have such a hard time giving anything back.

Our track record of behaviour, on the other hand, has not been as impressive. Sometimes, instead of bringing down our Father's favour, we bring his wrath. "And therefore will the Lord wait, that he may be gracious unto you and therefore will he be exalted, that he may have mercy upon you: for the Lord is a God of judgement; blessed are all they that wait for him" (Isaiah 30:18). Aren't you grateful he holds back on some things?

Be patient with your Father, as he is patient with you. "No good thing will he withhold from them that walk uprightly" (Psalm 84:11). Don't lose faith; remember that God will do what he said he will do. No matter how the situation looks, trust him still. One thing I know for sure is that every day I wake up, I'm one step closer to his promises being fulfilled in my life. He did not forget me. If you are going through your own "I-don't-trust-God" stage, perhaps you should review your relationship with him.

Process and Time

Everything is according to time and there is a process we must follow. It's a process that cannot be forced or manipulated by man. On the DVD case of Mel Gibson's movie, *Apocalypto,* it says, "No one can outrun their destiny." Moses soon found that to be true when he ran away from Egypt to Midian. The situation that caused him to make that decision was part of his process; he just didn't know it. His purpose in life was in the very place from which he ran.

Like Moses, many of us, as children of God, have been forced to run away from the place where our purpose is to be carried out. Some of us have this understanding, and others do not. Moses did not know that God had such a great purpose on his life when he ran away (and no one can speculate whether he would have made the same decision had he been privy to that knowledge). Jonah, on the other hand, outwardly disobeyed God. For that little stunt, he found himself in quite a predicament. Being disobedient to God has never worked out quite so well for anyone who dared to try, from Genesis to Revelation.

It is about process and timing for God, and there is no escaping it. Through any process, it is inevitable that one will go through difficulties and hardships. Do not ever be discouraged! Whatever you may be going through, trust that the Lord will work things out for your good. "And we know that all things work together for good to them that love God, to them who are the called according to his purpose" (Romans 8:28). Sometimes we cannot see how any situation that causes us discomfort and hardship could ever work out for our good, but I encourage you to only keep your faith in God.

I have a lot of respect for Joseph, the son of Jacob, whom the Bible speaks of in Genesis 37–50. Because of his practically flawless character, Joseph's suffering through his process typified him to be a type of Christ in his time. It is not that he was actually sinless (for he had within himself the same corrupt nature that any other child of Adam has). It pleased God to emphasize the faithfulness and practical godliness of his devoted servant rather than to speak of any flaws or blemish that his holy eye may have discerned.

If we should study Joseph as a type of Christ, we would first notice:

- he was the beloved of the Father's heart
- his many premonitions of coming glory
- how he sought out his brethren
- the rejection of the son
- the tale of the tempted one
- how he was exalted in glory
- his determination to "go to Jesus"

Although Joseph suffered a great deal through his process, he was afterward exalted and glorified because he remained faithful to the one whom he worshipped as his God. If we remain faithful to God, he will never let us down. You cannot change or alter the destiny or purpose God has chosen for you. Others may try to destroy you or hinder your purpose, but if it is God's will, it must be done. People may plot against you and do much wickedness to you to crush your spirit and stop your progress, but never forget that God always means good for you. If you have to run like Moses, run! Someday you will be called upon to accomplish the mission for which you have been destined.

For I reckon that the sufferings of this present time
are not worthy to be compared with the glory
which shall be revealed in us.
—Romans 8:18

Chapter 9

Fearing God

*I*f you are a genuine born-again follower of Jesus Christ, then you understand what I mean when I say there have been days when I have felt *oppressed, suppressed and* sometimes *depressed* by the troubles that have come my way until I learned God's Word. If you are experiencing similar feelings, do not worry, for you are not alone. The Word of God tells us that "Man that is born of a woman is of few days and full of trouble" (Job 14:1). "Many are the afflictions of the righteous; but the Lord delivers him out of them all" (Psalm 34:19).

The adversary is set up in all kinds of places to oppose and oppress God's people. This means that in your home, workplace or your place of worship, the enemy has been assigned to turn straws in your way and rise up against you. The enemies of your soul just do not want to see you bear fruits and become successful in God. Exodus 1 gives us a good understanding of this kind of trouble.

When the king of Egypt saw that the children of God were fruitful and multiplying abundantly, he became threatened and plotted to set taskmasters over them to afflict them with burdens. Romans 8:31 assures us that your enemies will not be successful because, "If God be for us, who can be against us?" Even though he is fighting a losing battle, the enemy will never give up trying to destroy you through any means necessary.

The king further gave instructions to the midwives to destroy the newborn baby boys so that they would stop increasing. How far is one willing to go to stop your progress? As you can see, the enemy is clearly willing to go as low as he possibly needs to in order to see your destruction.

This unfortunate truth really saddens me: most times, we are oppressed by those who claim to be people of God. Shortly after I got saved, I begin to realize how hard it was to find the right place of worship. I didn't go to the house of God to fight with anyone, but they clearly were fighting with me. I visited quite a few places, trying to find the right place until I received the revelation of God's Word. Like me, you may find the perfect place to worship, but not a perfect church.

The spirit of Pharaoh is very much operating in people today. As I have said, it is sad to know that believers are not exempt in being vessels for such a spirit. It is a jealous, hateful, controlling and vindictive spirit that hates to see progression. It will kill you if God is not on your side. I once heard a preacher compare the house of God to a hospital. He said it was a place where you go to be delivered or healed. But the harsh reality is it is also a place where you can be killed (spiritually, that is) if you let your guard down.

If you are pregnant with a purpose to bring change, you can be certain that the spirit of Pharaoh wants to kill it. He sees you as a threat to his position. Unless a true, God-fearing midwife is seeing you through your delivery, your purpose may not live. The lives of these newborn babies were spared because of the midwives' awareness and communal respect for God. Please understand that as a child of God, any enemy of God is an enemy of yours! They are determined to stop his purpose from fulfilling in our lives.

As told in Matthew 2, the story of King Herod and baby Jesus illustrates this fact well. When King Herod heard the prophecy of a child being born to rule over God's people, he became angry and immediately thought of ways to stop that prophecy from ever coming to pass. Had it not been for wise men that feared God, the outcome may have been different.

It is no wonder that King Solomon declared, "The fear of the Lord is the beginning of wisdom: and the knowledge of the holy is understanding" Proverbs 9:10. To fear God is to hold him in reverence. It means to respect, obey and submit to his discipline. Outside of that, you are open to being the devil's gofer. I encourage you to read the full story for yourself. Although Herod secretly wanted to kill Jesus, he behaved as though he wanted to celebrate him. Learn to read between the lines; not everyone who says they want the best for you actually means it. Some people who say, "I love you" don't mean it. The devil inside is actually saying, "I hate you, and I wish you were dead."

So that you can detect these wicked spirits, you need to stay close to the Lord and stay in his Word. When we have to do battle with such a spirit in those who are our spiritual leaders, it is especially frightening. Many of them, through their own misguided insecurities, incorrectly believe that they need to defend their positions. They don't. When you are confident God is with you, you will not have a need to defend your position; he will defend it for you. Your job is to nurture the purpose of those whom God has placed in your care, not to stifle and kill them.

When King Saul heard that David was anointed to be king over Israel, he immediately began to defend his position. He stopped at nothing to kill David's purpose. David would not have escaped had he not behaved wisely. In this situation, it is plain to see that unlike Saul, David was very much a God-fearing man. I am not afraid to speak boldly, so I will say it, hear clearly: *If you feel you have to kill another person's purpose to secure your own, God is not with you.* A genuine God-fearing person knows that you cannot fight against God and win. Whatever God wants to happen will happen, regardless of how hard you may fight it.

The kingdom of God is not about competing with others. We are not stars on the Broadway stage or in Hollywood movies, where we show off our outfits and accolades. We aren't invited there to take over or show off how gifted we are. We are here to learn the ways of royalty. We are here to be humble and gracious. Check your heart; make sure you are not someone the enemy can convince to participate in their grand scheme of destroying lives. Yield yourself as a vessel God is able to use. He wants you to deliver someone, not kill them.

> The fear of the Lord is to hate evil:
> pride, and arrogancy, and the evil way,
> and the forward mouth, do I hate.
> —Proverbs 8:13

Chapter 10

Don't Forget

*W*hen it comes to short-term memory loss, it's sad to say that as people of God, we are guilty as charged. No matter how many times the Lord helps us out of a situation; we never seem to remember that he did it. This causes us to suffer the same near-drowning panic experience each time we are faced with deep waters to cross. "Remember this day in which you come out from Egypt, out of the house of Bondage; for by strength of hand the Lord brought you out of this place" (Exodus 13:3).

In this same Scripture, he told them four times to remember but we don't remember, do we? It seems as though we've forgotten nearly everything the Lord has told us to do. Even worse than forgetting what He has told us to remember, we have forgotten God himself.

This sin of ungratefulness has destroyed the very thing we need to serve the Lord right: our minds. In Exodus 20:8, the Lord reminds us to keep the Sabbath day holy. It is very important to God; otherwise he would not have told us not to forget it. Whenever you are reminded to do something, it is to make certain that it gets carried out. The one commandment he says to remember is the one we have conveniently forgotten.

The truth is, no one wants to be forgotten; it's a terrible thing. Feelings of rejection, abandonment and disappointment surface when one suspects he has been forgotten. One of the criminals who was crucified alongside Jesus begged for Jesus not to forget him when he went back to his kingdom, and Jesus granted his plea. Jesus himself felt forsaken by his Father during his period of suffering on the cross—and understandably so. "My God, my God, why hast thou forsaken me?" (Matthew 27:46). We can all relate to that feeling of rejection, can't we?

Many times, when we are going through our test and trials, we have asked the same question of God the Father. "Have you forgotten me?" The thought of God forgetting us is terrifying, yet we do not consider how it makes God feel when we forget him or the things he tells us to do. It is because we have forgotten him that we suffer the illness of forgetfulness.

Forgetting causes us to conveniently rebel and disobey God's Word. Of course, no matter how convenient it may be for you, not all convenience is a blessing. Take your time and think about it. In 2 Corinthians 13:5, the apostle Paul admonished the church at Corinth. "Examine yourselves, whether ye be in the faith; prove your own selves." He asked them to honestly ascertain whether Christ was in them or not. There is no one better to examine your soul than yourself. The only way to do that is by revisiting God's Word.

Surrender your mind to God. Ask him to heal you, that you can once again remember. We have set aside a day to remember soldiers who have laid down their lives for their country. How much more should we set aside to honour the True and Living God who is responsible for giving us life?

Obey and Stay Blessed

When the Lord rains his blessings upon you, it's not for you to rebel against him and begin doing your own thing. Consider yourself and do the right things. It would seem to me that with God, every blessing has a test attached to it. In Exodus 16:4, the

Lord told Moses, "Behold, I will rain bread from heaven for you; and the people shall go out and gather a certain rate every day, that I may prove them, whether they will walk in my law, or no." God is still waiting for us to obey his laws.

The story of the biggest blessing ever put to the test was told in the book of Genesis. God made Adam and Eve and gave them everything to their human comfort. Yet there was a test attached. They were instructed, "But of the tree of knowledge of good and evil, thou shalt not eat of it; for in the day that thou eatest thereof thou shalt surely die" (Genesis 2:17). We all know they failed that test miserably. In 1 Samuel 15, the Lord blessed Saul as king to lead his people. He also was given instructions by the Lord, and he also failed miserably. There are many more examples such as these, where God blessed many people, still they failed in being obedient to him.

From Genesis to Revelation, you can find the consistency in man's failure to obey God. But we are not without hope. We have also seen many victories. A very interesting young man by the name of Joseph, whose life you can read about throughout Genesis 37–50, did what was right when his blessings and instructions faced him. Then there is our father Abraham, who, in Genesis 22, passed his test with flying colours. It makes you wonder where we would be today if he had failed his test too, doesn't it? I won't leave out my girl Esther, who received her own book in the Bible because of her obedience after her blessing.

Consider yourself when asking God for a blessing to rain upon you. It's not about the blessing; it's about what you do with it. You need to learn to walk in your blessing. If we don't obey God's laws after we receive his blessings, we are surely creating problems in our lives. The book of Deuteronomy cautions us of the curse of our disobedience and the blessing of our obedience. Since we are now under the law of grace, we sometimes forget that rules and principles are still very much a part of God's kingdom.

The rules of blessings and curses are quite simple, really. Much of the outcome has to do with us playing our part. God only cautions us of the danger that could befall us should we go outside the boundaries of these guidelines. Say that someone cautioned you not to climb over a certain wall because you would be bitten by a dog if you did. If you disobeyed that advice and did it anyway (and were, as promised, bitten by the dog), who do you think is the real cause of your misfortune? (You are.)

It all comes down to trust. When we trust, we obey. It is actually quite dangerous not to trust God. Considering our human tendency to malfunction, I can see where you would have a problem trusting another human. There is, however, absolutely no reason for you to mistrust God. He is the creator of all things made without hands. He is omniscient, omnipresent and omnipotent. If you have never trusted anyone in your lifetime, learn to trust God. Your blessing is in your obedience, so obey and stay blessed!

Although King Saul outwardly disobeyed God's command to him, he then went and made a sacrifice unto him. This was not a sacrifice in obedience, but one in disobedience. The prophet Samuel told King Saul, "To obey is better than sacrifice" (1 Samuel 15:22). Give yourself a challenge; find out why obedience is better than an offering to God.

> All these blessings shall come on you,
> and overtake you,
> if you will listen to the voice of the Lord your God.
> —Deuteronomy 28:2

Chapter 11

Resurrected Discipline

"*H*e that curses his father, or his mother, shall surely be put to death" (Exodus 21:17).

Let me take this time to talk about our young people of today. After all, they are our future. We must acknowledge this and protect their God-given inheritance. Let's consider the awesomeness of God's grace. We are no longer subjected to stiff penalties for our sins, but I just can't help worrying that newer generations are missing the message here. Perhaps our teenage crime rate would not have escalated to this degree in which it has if today's youth truly lived by Exodus 21:17.

Although God may have been merciful enough to exempt this law, there are many biblical disciplinary laws from which we are not exempt. For example, Exodus 20:12 tells us to honour our father that our days may be long upon the land, which the Lord our God have given us. Is it mere coincidence that our children's lives are being cut short? I think not. We have not regarded God's laws as correct discipline for our children. Therefore, we have changed them to suit our own folly. The result of which has left our children to suffer the curse that comes through disobeying God's Word.

Is what is happening to our children the result of our own rebellion against our heavenly Father? By removing the laws of

God from our homes, we have taken away their hope for long life and a better future. God said it: long life can be obtained through honouring your parents. It is so heartrending to see parents entertaining their children's bad behaviour.

Once again, the enemy has disarmed us. We are privy to watch our children being carted off to prison or the morgue, all because we have formed mischief against God's Word by the laws of our so-called society. We are instead trained to ignore God's wisdom on raising his own creations. Proverbs 13:24 says, "He that spares his rod hates his son: but he who loves him is careful to discipline him." But society warns us that if we use the rod, it's off to jail we go. The devil is a liar. It's time for us to rise up and protest against these laws that are an obvious device to shorten our children's lives. We are so backwards and blind. We protest when we are not getting enough money on our precious jobs, but when it comes to what benefits our children in saving their lives, we are laid back and complacent with it. Why is that?

We are not capable of passing on the wisdom of God's Word to our children if we ourselves do not possess it. Proverbs 10:1 says, "A wise son maketh a glad father: but a foolish son is the heaviness of his mother." How many mothers are left mourning their children's death because of the unwise decision of themselves or another? The Word of God is a lifesaver if we just take the time to seek out its treasures.

Just reading the book of Proverbs alone would change the course of one's life for the better, from despair to hope, from darkness to light and from sadness to joy.

For example, there are thirty-one chapters in this book. Think about this: you could have a completely new life in one month just by taking the time to read one chapter every day! Prove it; it's a straightforward manual with easy-to- understand basic instructions to practical, everyday living.

Consider how much time you spend watching television and reading bad news in the newspapers or magazines filled with garbage. There is absolutely nothing to help you with the responsibility of parenting. Parenting is above every job in the universe. The principles you instill in your children now determine the adults they will soon be.

This is something every mother should know. Any good doctor will advise you that as far as food goes, breast milk is one of the best things a mother can offer her newborn child. It provides the child with basic nutrition during the first months of life, which will set the pace for optimum health throughout life. There are three different stages to a woman's breast milk: colostrum, transitional milk and mature milk.

Colostrum is the first and most important part of the milk. It is packed with all the nutrients to develop a healthy baby. Apparently it is so high in antibodies that some say it is the baby's first immunization. It includes everything a baby needs to fight off bacteria and disease. (Still think God doesn't know what he is doing?)

Transitional and mature milk is still healthy. It comes out in larger quantity than the colostrum but features fewer nutrients. Most of this milk is for the growth and weight of the baby. As it is with the natural, so it is with the spiritual. The best thing you can give your child in the early stages of their life is the Word of God. There is nothing better for them. Just reading them a good storybook and singing to them is not good enough. It's really more like giving your child processed milk instead of the real thing.

The first epistle of Peter makes an interesting comparison. Just as newborn babies desire the sincere milk of their mothers to grow, so should we desire the Word of God. We were made to live by God's Word, not just natural food. "Man shall not live by bread alone, but by every word that proceeds out of the mouth of God" (Deuteronomy 8:3).

This may be the reason why we are so sick. There are millions of people sick and dying of disease every day. Some diseases are called "rare" because they cannot be explained. These are just disease that sin breathes. Our souls are lacking the nutrients that the Word of God contains. The sickness inside our bodies is just a manifestation of what is taking place in our soul.

According to God's Word, we partake of foods that are considered unclean both naturally and spiritually. There is no counteraction for the bacteria that it releases in us. The Word of God is designed to nurture, nourish and heal us. Think about it: if the doctor told you that you have a deadly disease and that Tylenol would cure it, would you not take it? Sure you would! Most people would; we are taught to trust our doctors.

Now think of sin as that deadly disease and the Word of God as Tylenol. If we can trust a man simply because of his profession, why can't we trust the God who made him? This pill may be hard for a lot of us to swallow, but may I suggest taking it any way you can? Otherwise, you risk slow, daily depletion. One day, you will be so sick in your soul that you won't have a fighting chance. God's Word is not only nourishment for you, it is also for your children. Stop eating "junk food" now. You are killing yourself and your children, body and soul.

> Now no chastening for the present seems to be joyous,
> but grievous: nevertheless afterward it yieldeth
> the peaceable fruit of righteousness
> unto them which are exercised thereby.
> —Hebrews 12: 11

Chapter 12

Yes, Lord!

"And Moses spoke before the Lord, saying, behold the children of Israel have not hearkened unto me; how then shall Pharaoh hear me, who am of uncircumcised lips?" (Exodus 6:12). "And Moses said before the Lord, behold, I am of uncircumcised lips and how shall Pharaoh hearken unto me?" (Exodus 6:30).

Why are we so much like Moses today? We're still full of excuses and reluctance to do what God asks us to do. Is it because of our fear for people and thinking we are not good enough? Twice in the same chapter, Moses points out to God he's of uncircumcised lips. You don't need to remind God of your shortcomings, he knows what they are. After all, he made you.

Although many would consider Moses's response to be that of humility, God's reply showed that Moses was yet ignorant of just how powerful God really is. It is humble to acknowledge our sins to God, but not our inadequacies; he already knows all about our capabilities. Furthermore, it's not our abilities that gets the job done; it is the power of God working through us.

God doesn't choose you for a task because of your adequacies; he ordained you for that purpose before the foundations of the earth. Besides, he does whatever pleases him. Your life has been carefully planned out. You are just a part of his grand master plan.

From the day you were born, you have been being groomed and trained for your big day, this is done through your tests and trials, so even when you mess up and somehow stray off the path, he's still able to work it out that his will is accomplished. God has placed something in you that he will use when he is ready, not when you are ready.

Never mind the impertinence of anyone who thinks they know more than God; they are just tools being used to hinder your purpose. Show up with your imperfections with a willing and humble heart and see what God does. This is not encouragement to stay that way, but it will help you to see the perfectness and the power of God. When God commands you to do something, your only answer should be, "Lord, what will You have me to do? Despite the fact I may be a murderer, despite the fact I may be a liar, despite the fact I may be a thief. Here I am, Lord. Let your will be done."

The following is but one of the reasons I admire Paul the apostle (before his conversion in Acts 9) is this. While he was on his way to Damascus to persecute the disciples of the Lord, he had his encounter with God. He did not point out to the Lord who he was. He was smart enough to know that Almighty God already knew all about him before he stopped him in his tracks in such powerful way. With trembling and astonishment, Paul simply said, "Lord, what will you have me to do?" If we adopt this same attitude, we will be able to powerfully do the work of the Lord, just as Paul was able to do.

Here you can observe the difference between these two great men of God. Although we can all be used mightily by God, some of us may need a little bit more convincing before we get started on our chosen calling or purpose. Believe that when you have the ability to recognize when the power of Almighty God is operating, you will become a lot less reluctant to believe in the abilities he has placed within you.

Work of Excellence

When you have been given a project by God, he is expecting it to be carried out just as he has instructed you, without any alterations. In Exodus 26:30, God told Moses to build up the tabernacle according to the fashion that was shown to him on the mountain. God is very precise, perfect and excellent in all his ways. Therefore whatever we do in representation of him should also have the mark of excellence on it.

It is no wonder that Psalm 127:1 declares, "Except the Lord build the house they labour in vain that build it." It is so evident that this vital piece of information is no longer a consideration in our building plan. It is more an attitude. "Well, God," we might say, "I hope you like it, because I am doing it in your name. If you don't, oh well, I'll be moving right along!" This type of attitude is exactly what will land us right in the line of Matthew 7:23: "I never knew you: depart from me, you that work iniquity. Oh, yes, it is iniquity to not care or value God's opinion on something you're doing in his own name. Man would not stand for this. Imagine the supreme God being in acceptance of this gutter mentality? No wonder so many so-called ministers fail to accomplish what they start!

Whatever you are doing in the Lord's name, whether big or small, must be nothing less than excellent. In Zechariah 4:10, the Lord asks, "Who has despised the day of small things?" God doesn't start you off with big things. He watches to see how faithful you will be over the small things. In Matthew 25:21, Jesus told of the servant who did the best he could over the few things he was given to do, and how it pleased the Lord to reward him.

Very few people seem to care about being rewarded later. They are only interested in what they are able to get now. *Later* for them is too much expectation of faith. It's time we get our act together. If you are truly chosen by God to be in service for him, then you will not make it all about you. You will spend time in his presence trying to get the blueprint to build whatsoever you have envisioned to do for him. He will honour it when he sees your good desire is coming from a clean heart.

God wants your vision to come through. He wants you to be successful. In fact, Proverbs 29:18 says, "Where there is no vision, the people perish." He is waiting for you to bring your vision to him. Proverbs 3:6 tells you to acknowledge him in all your ways and he will direct your path. As you can see, in Exodus 26, the Lord was very keen on details, the very curtains for the tabernacle he designed to his liking. Know that God is original; he is no copycat. No matter how small the project is, it should have people standing in awe of him! They must say God is in it.

Attention to Details

It is not acceptable that we just get up and build without purpose. When we are building without purpose, we tend to be very sloppy. As I read through Exodus 37, I realized that God is very precise in purpose. No single detail should be missing from the instructions that you have been given. In Genesis, when God gave Noah instructions to build the ark, he was very specific in them.

Just what might have happened if Noah had disobeyed God? What if Noah decided that he didn't think it necessary to put a window right there? Why does the door have to be at the side? Why does the length have to be exactly three hundred cubits? What would have happened if he just questioned everything God said? How would that have worked out for us today? But the Scriptures said repeatedly that Noah did according to all that God commanded him.

Sometimes the Lord gives us some specific instructions. At the time, these can even be (if I may boldly say) silly. But believe it or not, that's when you know that it's him. The way in which God does things is not to be understood by simple human minds. His ways and his thoughts surpasses ours. His Word tells us that his wisdom is foolishness to us; likewise, our wisdom is foolishness to him.

It was that very understanding, that inspired one of the most profound conversation Jesus has ever had with his disciples, Jesus asked, "Whom say ye that I am?" Simon Peter answered and said. "Thou art the Christ, the Son of the living God." Jesus answered and said unto him, Blessed art thou, Simon Barjona: For flesh and blood hath not reveal it unto thee, but my father which is in heaven (Matthew 16:15-17). So it is, when you are given a task by the Lord, it is to be done through the Spirit of God. Your own human self alone cannot accomplish it.

People who are chosen to carry out specific tasks from the Lord are chosen according to the abilities God himself has placed within them. You cannot start a task then decide that it is too hard or that it is taking too long. God chooses you based on your ability for completion, not only starting. He has never started anything he is not able to finish, so it should be with us. The apostle Paul said, "Being confident of this very thing, that he which hath begun a good work in you will perform it until the day of Jesus Christ" (Philippians 1:6). Don't be discouraged or concerned if it seems as though God is not working in your life anymore; he is.

Consider a person who carves things out of wood and the work it requires from start to finish: cutting, carving, sanding, detailing, varnishing. It's a lot of work, not to be accomplished in one day. The work must be up to the retailer's standard. Otherwise, it would not be accepted. Every detail counts.

This is why people who gossip always make a mess of things. They are rarely detail-oriented; there is always some piece of information missing. They are sloppy people who just want to get it out there without caring how it looks. If we are aiming to produce an excellent finished product (meaning ourselves), God doesn't do sloppy and neither should we.

> And God saw everything that he had made,
> and behold, it was very good.
> —Genesis 1:31

Chapter 13

Spiritual Work

*T*he oldest deception in the book concerning work is found in Exodus 5:8: "And the tale of bricks, which they did make previously, you shall lay upon them; you shall not diminish ought thereof: for they be idle; therefore they cry saying let us go and sacrifice to our God." Exodus 5:17 adds, "But he said you are idle, you are idle: therefore you say, let us go and sacrifice to the Lord."

Pharaoh's only concern was to meet his daily quota. He was not about to give the people of God time out to go and worship. After all, he knew not God to honour his request. How has that changed in our modern-day world? Consider the "slave-driving" boss who resists your requests for a measly half hour out from their busy work so you can pray, an action that could save your life (or that of another). What we give to the Lord is always what is left over, isn't it? Our time is consumed with working eight or more hours in a day, after which we turn to the duties of our homes and other extracurricular activities we have engaged ourselves in.

In today's society, God's people are still seen as idlers, unproductive losers. As long as we are not spending our time being burdened down with Pharaoh's work, we are then counted as nothing. Slavery has become fashionable. It is hidden behind big degrees, three-piece suits, fancy buildings, nice offices, and prestigious titles. If you can't cut it in that group, you should consider yourselves privileged. After all, you're lucky enough to have a job, right? You are allowed to work your fingers to the bone in some factory in order to earn only enough money to get by from day to day, paycheque to paycheque. And the cycle continues. This daily drama leaves you with only enough time to cry out to God for deliverance.

When God answers your prayers and calls you into his employment, then comes the old deceiver again to tell you that you are a bum. If you are not strong enough to handle criticisms such as these, do not ask God for his help. No matter what, it still beats suffering through Pharaoh's oppression. He's good at making people feel as though doing anything for God is a waste of your time, which as we know couldn't be further from the truth. You just have to get to the place in your mind where the opinions of others do not affect you. It's that or get comfortable living as Pharaoh's beast of burden.

The second verse of a gospel song titled "Close To Thee" says:

> *"Not for ease or worldly pleasure,*
> *nor for fame my prayer shall be;*
> *gladly will I toil and suffer, only let me walk with thee."*

For whom would you prefer to suffer, God or man? In 1 Corinthians 9:1, the apostle Paul asked, "Am I not an apostle? Am I not free? Have I not seen Jesus Christ our Lord? Are you not my work in the Lord?"

If you examine 1 Corinthians 9 in its entirety, you'll see where Paul was teaching that work is work, whether spiritual or natural. "If we have sown unto you spiritual things, Is it a great thing if we shall reap your carnal things?" (1 Corinthians 9:11). Paul just wants the same respect as the man in the suit. You don't have to give him a thing if you so desire. Paul knows his God will supply his every need through whomever or whatever method he pleases (Philippians 4:19).

"The just shall live by faith" (Hebrews 10:38). Let's respect each other. I won't criticize your work if you won't criticize mine. Now before you walk away misunderstanding me, let me make myself clear: There is nothing wrong with great education, big degrees, and sophisticated jobs. These can all be profitable in this life. We should pursue them; however, nothing is more profitable than what you do for the Lord. Do not be utterly consumed with achieving things that will eventually perish. Spare yourself some time to be educated in the things of God that are eternal.

Getting Paid

It is not going to be an easy time when you begin the work of the Lord; oppositions will always try to find a way to counteract what you set out to do. Yes, it can be discouraging and frustrating, but the important thing is not to give up. It is only the grace of God that allows us to carry out any mission pertaining to him. There is always a blessing to receive upon the completion of your work, even if the enemy tries hard to be a hindering force to that blessing.

"And Moses looked upon all the work and behold, they had done it as the Lord commanded, even so had they done it and Moses blessed them" (Exodus 39:43). It is no different from doing secular work. Upon the completion of your work, you will be paid. Whatever payment was agreed upon shall be given to you; anything else would be considered unjust. A workman is worthy of his pay. Many times, we are expecting to be blessed by the Lord without doing the thing that we are commissioned to do.

In the New Testament, from Matthew to John, Jesus repeatedly made reference to doing his Father's work. He knew about the crown that awaited him and therefore maintained his focus. No one works without expecting to receive a reward at the end. Proverbs 24:12 says, "God shall render to every man according to his works." God is not partial in his blessings. It is not about your job being great or small or the many hours that you put in.

God is about equality. What matters to him is that you don't give up doing what you've started for him.

It is not God's desire to hold on to what he promises, but there is a big part we play in that release. Just what kind of blessing have you been expecting from God that you have not yet received? Now ask yourself, "What is it that I am to do for him that I have not yet done?" You have heard many times of a blessing being delayed, but not denied, and while there is truth in that, there is always a reason for the delay, whether it is on your part or some other force, seen or unseen.

Sometimes you may be running late with the task that has been set before you, or you have decided to take a break. Whatever the circumstances, it all boils down to how badly you need that blessing. It is that desperation that will become the driving force for the completion of that work. Consider the blessing that awaits you and get back to the unfinished work.

Until It's Finished

Think about this today: How much easier would things go in the world of ministry if we were all equally dedicated to the work of the Lord? What if more of us focused on that mission? What if we did our part to inspire those workers to work for the Lord, not their own personal gain? It's not to impress the pastor or someone else in the congregation, but through a faithful and dedicated heart, we can accomplish the will of God. We must be careful that we are not doing the right thing for the wrong reason. In Exodus 38:22, it says that Bezaleel (the son of Uri, the son of Hur of the tribe of Judah) made all that the Lord commanded Moses.

As great of a leader as Moses was, the passage did not say all that Moses commanded them. It says that the Lord commanded Moses. These were obviously men of understanding. Your focus in ministry should be to carry out all that God expects you to do. Don't worry about what anyone else wants of you. Respect your leader enough to not fight against him in carrying out the will of

God. Lose yourself; it's not about you. Many times ministries are laid waste because we cannot come to the understanding that we are doing God's work, not ours.

Has this happened to you? You declare that you are *starting* a work for the Lord, but you stop before it is completed. Why? It has already been tried and proven that there is no task that we set out to do for the Lord that the enemy will not oppose. But that's no reason to just throw up your arms and call it defeat! No! God's children are more than conquerors through our Lord Jesus Christ. Greater is he that is in us than he that is in the world. Let no man stop you from doing what you've set out to do for the Lord. Because of their determination to finish what they started for the Lord, in spite of strong opposition, Nehemiah and his workers are an encouragement to us throughout generations.

Nehemiah 6:2-4 tells us, "That San-bal'-at and Ge'-shem sent word to him, saying that they wanted to meet with him in some one of the villages in the plain of O'-no, but they thought to do him mischief, and he sent messengers unto them saying, I am doing a great work, so that I cannot come down: why should the work cease, while I leave it and come down to you? Yet they sent unto him four times after this sort; and he answered them after the same manner."

When you're doing God's work, it should be considered as nothing less than a great thing. It's not just "any old job." You should always put your best foot forward, as the phrase goes. Keep your focus and don't let anyone bring you down with their negative thinking, words or behaviour. Like Nehemiah and Bezaleel and Uri, don't stop the work you've started for the Lord until it's finished. God doesn't do anything halfway and neither should we.

> Thus the heavens and the earth were finished,
> and all the host of them.
> —Genesis 2:1

Chapter 14

Your Sacrifice

*T*hanks to false doctrine being preached, people have been under the wrong impression for a while now. They think that in order to serve God, you must get rid of everything that is considered as "bad" in our eyes. News flash! You can never get rid of any worldly attachments or ways without God's help. If we were allowed to choose our sacrifices, we would not be truly making one. No human being is really willing to give up the things that are pleasurable to him, unless God asks him to.

When given, a true sacrifice is something that must be felt from the depths of your soul. You must have a heart that has truly repented before you decide to accept the call of the Lord, otherwise the Lord's request will become a struggle for you. Sacrifices to the true and living God are for those who are born again, because the sins we take the most pleasure in are in the body.

The Lord requires a sacrifice so that he might have a clean vessel to use. That's why the apostle Paul appeals to the people of God in Romans 12:1: "I beseech you brethren, by the mercies of God, that he present your bodies a living sacrifice holy and acceptable unto God, which is your reasonable service."

This can only be honoured if you have truly made God your all-in-all. This God so beautifully demonstrates this to us in

Genesis 22. He called Abraham and commanded him to sacrifice his only son, but before it was too late, he stopped Abraham and provided him with a ram instead. In this, he shows us that in our willingness to sacrifice the things we love, he already has made provisions to replace them. God doesn't leave anything void. When we are asked to sacrifice our *body*, He is not asking for us to destroy the flesh but the deed that have been done with it.

I believe that because Abraham came from a culture where they worshipped idols, God tested him to see if those ways were still in him. It would not be hard for Abraham to idolize the child he had with the love of his life (a sin many of God's people are guilty of). We need to give these things to God. The sacrifice may be painful, but it's still better than allowing sin to destroy your body.

So come to the Lord truly today. Come as you are. Bring everything, and he will do the sorting. As Moses said to Pharaoh in Exodus 10:26, "Our cattle also shall go with us; there shall not a hoof be left behind; for thereof must we take to serve the Lord our God; and we know not with what we must serve the Lord, until we get there." You don't have to get rid of a thing to please God. Just go to the Lord with a willing and repented heart, and he will help you to sort out what is valuable to keep.

A good example of this is Paul the apostle. Before his conversion, he killed many of the followers of Christ. Did God stop him? Did he say, "I need you to serve me and stop killing people?" No! He simply made Paul realize that he was passionate about the wrong things and that he was on the wrong team.

God turned Paul's passion for killing into a passion for preaching. Now, Paul saved lives instead of destroying them. Go to the Lord with everything, and he will tell you what to give up. Don't let anyone make you give up what you will need to worship the Lord.

Willing Offering

God is expecting us to give to him from a willing heart always. We are not doing him any favour by doing otherwise. God has given to us willingly of everything he owns. The earth is the Lord's and the fullness thereof, the world and they that dwell therein. We belong to him. Everything we own (and therefore, things we should be willing to give to him) is whatever he blesses us to partake of, however small the portion we may be holding.

When we give to the Lord willingly, we can ask him without guilt to increase the portion we have been given. Acts 20:35 tells us it is better to give than to receive. Freely give and freely he shall receive. It is never a good decision to withhold anything from God, by choosing not to do the things God requires of us. We are only blessed to give, and should consider it a privilege to be able to be a blessing to others.

I admonish you now not to be ignorant. Many times, preachers want us to believe that only our cold, hard cash can get God's attention. I am not saying that you shouldn't give of your money to God, but when you have to be poked and prodded to do so, there is no blessing to receive from that. God is not only expecting you to give back of your finances, he expects you to freely give any and all gifts he has blessed you with; he is expecting you to bless others *willingly*.

We withhold from God with our praise and worship, reading, praying, etc. Whatever ability the Lord has given to you, don't be afraid to share it. Bless others with the gifts God has given you, in all things and in all ways.

In the Bible, we read of the people of God who came together willingly and gave to the work of God for his glory. Are you the kind of person who gives willingly or sparingly? As 2 Corinthians 9:6–7 tells us, "he which sowed bountifully shall reap bountifully. Every man according as he purposed in his heart, so let him give; not grudgingly, or of necessity; for God loves a cheerful giver."

The condition of your heart is the key to a willing offering. A person who is willing to give from her heart is a cheerful giver. This is not necessarily the kind of cheerful demonstration for the benefit of man; it is the cheerfulness of giving to the Lord.

When monetary offerings are being collected in the house of the Lord, I have witnessed the demonstration of unhappy giving. It is there in the body language, the sad faces and the clenched fists. These givers simply give because they are man-pleasers, not God-pleasers. They are more concerned about *looking* good, instead of *doing* good. "If I don't give something," these people ask, "what will people think?" So they painfully reach for the smallest of offering to give, although they are thoroughly furnished to bless the church with much more.

It makes no difference whether your offering is a penny or a thousand dollars. Without the right heart attached to the number, you are giving in vain. Do you know the story of the widow's two mites?

> And he looked up, and saw the rich men putting their gifts into the treasury. And he saw also a certain poor widow putting in two mites and he said, of a truth I say unto you, that this poor widow hath put in more than they all. For all these have of their abundance cast in unto the offerings of God; but all she of her penury hath put in all the living that she had. (Luke 21:1–4)

Wait! Is this about faith? Are willing offerings all about faith? If those big spenders were in the same position as this widow, would they have had the faith to do what she did? Think about it and see what you come up with. If you give cheerfully out of the little that you have, you are richer than you think. If you give sparingly out of your abundance, you are poorer than you think.

Blessings Overflow

The wise men spoke to Moses, saying, "The people bring much more than enough for the service of the work, which the Lord commanded to make, and Moses gave commandment and they caused it to be proclaimed throughout the camp saying, let neither man nor woman make anymore work for the offering of the sanctuary."

So the people were restrained from bringing; the stuff they had was sufficient for all the work to make it and too much. Is this just me who finds this troubling? Never in my lifetime have I ever heard of people being restrained from bringing stuff to contribute to the work of the Lord. In fact, it is quite the opposite in these times we are living in.

If you ever want to see church folks change, just tell them that they need to give for the establishment of the work of the Lord. The spirit of giving seems to have gone away from us. By refusing to give back to the source from which our blessings flow, we are left with the problems we have created. When you give to the Lord from your heart, it should never be hard. What those people brought to contribute was more than enough, because it came from them willingly.

When you refuse to give to the work of God's ministry, know this: whatever you are holding on to, the Lord could take away from you. We have too often heard preachers reference Malachi 3:8–11 incorrectly:

> Will a man rob God? Yet ye have robbed me. But ye say, Wherein have we robbed thee? In tithes and offerings.
>
> Ye are cursed with a curse: for ye have robbed me, even this whole nation.

Bring ye all the tithes into the storehouse, that there may be meat in mine house, and prove me now herewith, saith the LORD of hosts, if I will not open you the windows of heaven, and pour you out a blessing, that there shall not be room enough to receive it.

And I will rebuke the devourer for your sakes, and he shall not destroy the fruits of your ground; neither shall your vine cast her fruit before the time in the field, saith the LORD of hosts.

These preachers use Malachi to get what *they* want out of God's people. however, it doesn't make it any less the truth as God said it, and still requires it from us.

Instead, consider Malachi 3:6–12: "For I am the Lord, I change not; therefore ye sons of Jacob are not consumed. Even from the days of your fathers ye have gone away from mine ordinances, and will return unto you said the Lord of host, but he said, when shall we return? Will a man rob God? Yet have ye robbed me, but you say wherein have we robbed thee? In tithes and offerings, you are cursed with a curse for you have robbed me, even this whole nation.

"Bring ye all the tithes into the storehouse that there may be meet in mine house, and prove me now herewith said the Lord of host If I will not open you the windows of heaven and pour you out a blessing; that there shall not be room enough to receive it." As it has been demonstrated by the people in Exodus 36, God's Word is obviously true. It profits you nothing to hold on to God's portion. When you do so, you are doing yourself great injustice. Take a moment to look up what James 5:1–7 says about this.

Chapter 15

All of Us

$\mathcal{I}$t is no wonder that we have not been able to follow the ways of the Lord the way we should as children of God, or receive his blessing the way we should. Without unity among us, there is very little that can be achieved in our aim to carry out the work of the Lord. I am in no position to lay blame on either sheep or shepherd if a leader believes he has a direct word from the Lord for the people. It would be better conveyed when all the members are present, to encourage them to come together on this occasion.

So that no individual is omitted from receiving blessings, it is important for us to stay close-knitted as members of our faith-filled communities. I am not talking about the people who drop in at random, but rather the dedicated men and women who have committed themselves to the ministry of building the kingdom of God. I cannot imagine why it would be so difficult for us to come together, if we truly have the work of the Lord on our minds.

We gather together for things concerning our own pleasures, yet when we are called to meet for the Lord's business, only a few of us show up. What can truly be accomplished this way? We keep trying to do things halfway, *our* way, only to get lost from God's way.

"And Moses gathered all the congregation of the children of Israel together, and said unto them. These are the words which the

Lord has commanded that you should do them" (Exodus 35:1–4). Which do you think is more likely? God has stopped giving direct word to our leaders anymore, or we have stopped following his orders? Too many of our congregational problems derive from us not being on one accord.

There is something about everyone receiving the Word at the same time. The day of Pentecost as recorded in Acts 2:1 says, "And when the day of Pentecost was fully come." When they were all in one accord in the same place, the Lord poured out his Holy Spirit on them. As a congregation, it is hard for us to receive the fullness of the Lord with just a part of the body present. It is impossible for a body that is missing parts to function to its fullest capability. Ephesians 4:10 clearly outlines what God is trying to accomplish with his church:

> He that descended is the same also that ascended up far above all heavens that he might fill all things. And he gave some apostles and some prophets and some evangelists and some pastors and teachers. For the perfecting of the saints, for the work of the ministry for the edifying of the body of Christ, till we all come in the unity of the faith and of the knowledge of the Son of God, unto a perfect man, unto the measure of the stature of the fullness of Christ that we henceforth be no more children tossed to and fro and carried about with every wind of doctrine by the sleight of men and cunning craftiness, whereby they lie in wait to deceive. Let us not be one of those who are deceived.

The only way to accomplish the will of God for his church is by all of us coming together in unity. There is no other way.

Be Kind to One Another

"You shall not oppress a stranger: as you know the heart of a stranger; seeing you were strangers in the Land of Egypt," said Moses to the people in Exodus 23:9, something that we all, as people of God, seem to conveniently forget. On more than one occasion, I have been oppressed by church folks who didn't think I was "worthy" enough to be called a child of God.

When I just got saved, there were many people in the house of the Lord who did not welcome me because I didn't look or behave the same as they. They forgot that before they were saved, they themselves were once sinners too. The Lord is simply reminding us not to forget where we are coming from and that it isn't through our own merits that we ourselves are no longer considered to be strangers.

A stranger is not just a person unknown to us by appearance or acquaintanceship, but more importantly one who is estranged from the Creator through sin. First Chronicles 29:15 says, "For we are strangers before thee and sojourners, as were all our fathers: our days on earth are as a shadow and there is none abiding."

Although we may be strangers, we share the same experiences in common. Therefore, we should not have a hard time relating to each other. You know what it's like to be a slave to sin. But since your deliverance, you've gotten so high minded that God himself is not able to reach you.

"I forgot" should not be used as a crutch to excuse bad behaviour towards each other. Being human is exactly the quality that should rev up our engines to take others along in our vehicle of understanding.

We should not need to be reminded to be loving towards each other, yet some of us need nudging to do so. Considering that you yourself received the same love and compassion from Jesus Christ, this should be a reflex for a child of God. People think that Jesus said, "Do unto others as you would have them do unto you," but this is actually paraphrased from Luke 6:31 ("As ye would that men should do to you, do ye also to them likewise"). This particular Scripture is as misquoted as it is misunderstood. Jesus is saying that whatever you would not like for yourself, do not do it to another, regardless of their colour, race or religion, as tempting as it may be. Hebrews 13:2 reminds us to always be hospitable: "Be not forgetful to entertain strangers: for thereby some have entertained angels unawares." I just want you to know that as believers, we will be tested.

One day, shortly after I got saved, as I was driving along a street in my neighbourhood, I approached a bus stop. I noticed a lady who was standing there alone with bags in her hands. Suddenly, I felt the need to stop and offer her a ride, so I did. We introduced ourselves, and as we conversed, I felt a great sense of peace.

I asked her where she was going, and she gave me the address of an apartment building about fifteen minutes from where I picked her up. Before she came out of the vehicle, she thanked me once again. I honestly can give no account of her. Whether she went into the building or behind the building, I do not know. Her actions were so swift, I missed it all. I have never seen her again and probably wouldn't recognize her, because I have no description of her face.

Another time, after grocery shopping, I came out of the store, put my groceries in the car, and prepared to go home, just like any other day. But on this day, I had an urge to go and pick up some glue at the dollar store. As I headed back to my vehicle, a lady asked if she could borrow my phone to make a quick call. She explained that she had accidentally locked her keys in her trunk. With no hesitation, I gave my phone to her. She made numerous attempts to call her home for help, but her husband clearly wasn't going to answer a call from a strange telephone number. I volunteered to take her home to get her spare keys, but she thought that was too much to ask of a stranger. I practically *forced* my goodwill on her.

After my insistence, she gave in and I drove her right to her door. She said she was a school teacher and expressed her gratitude for my kindness. I couldn't help but to think that sowing a seed into a teacher's life is good investment for our children. Later, she sent me a text thanking me again. "It's nice to know there are still decent people in this world of ours."

We should show kindness not just to those who believe, but those who are not believers also. Proverbs 11:30 tells us, "The fruit of the righteous is a tree of life; and he that winneth souls is wise." A righteous person is not only humble enough to want to save his own soul, he is also wise enough to want to save the souls of others. Instead, how many of us have damaged the souls of people, both in and outside of the church?

Be kind to people; you never know what kind of impression you may leave with them. It may bring restoration to a damaged soul. Your kindness may cause them to think of God, whom they have forgotten. In Matthew 5:16, Jesus said, "Let your light so shine before men, that they may see your good works and glorify your Father which is in heaven."

There are many things that we take for granted. We have no respect for the spirit of God within each other. When we dismiss others as not good enough or not up to our standards, we insult the spirit of God. We also judge people only because of their material possessions or social status, something we should never do.

We ought to be thankful that we have been redeemed through the grace of God and that same grace should be reflected in our attitudes towards another stranger. You should never be partial in who you show kindness to regardless of status, race, colour, language or religion. Whether they are morally or spiritually wrong, always put your best forward. Remember that your light could help someone who is lost find their way home.

> Let not mercy and truth forsake thee:
> bind them about thy neck; write them
> upon the table of thine heart: so shall thou
> find favour and good understanding
> in the sight of God and man.
> —Proverbs 3:3–4

Chapter 16

The Lord Your God

"They shall know that I am the Lord their God, that brought them out of the land of Egypt. That I may dwell among them: I am the Lord their God" (Exodus 29:46). There are many different types of religion in the world today, and many have their own beliefs about who God really is and why they should worship him. As for me, I am leaning toward the God who has proven himself to be the Creator of everything. There is only one God who has proven himself as a deliverer, provider and protector. Do you know the Lord your God? Do you know who he is? Who or what do you really believe? Are you worshipping a god who is not the Lord?

In Psalm 115, the psalmist cried out to God to answer the pagans who worshipped idols. The pagans taunted the people of God by saying, "Where is now their God?" He went on to say our God is in the heavens; he has done whatever he pleases. He pointed out the absurdity of their idolatry by saying, "their idols are silver and gold, the work of men's hands. They have mouth, but they speak not: eyes have they; but they see not. They have ears, but they hear not: noses have they, but they smell not. They have hands, but they handle not: feet have they, but they walk not: neither do they speak through their throat. They that make them are like unto them; so is everyone that trust in them."

If your god is not the Lord, you are obviously putting your trust in something that is not real. It seems crazy, doesn't it, to be praying to someone or something who doesn't respond? Think about it. It just doesn't add up! The Lord our God has sent out an invitation to us in Jeremiah 33:2–3: "Thus said the Lord, the maker thereof, the Lord that formed it, to establish it; the Lord is his name; call unto me, and I will answer you and show you great and mighty things, which you know not."

The Lord is inviting you to get to know him, something you should consider a great honour. You need to get to know your Creator. It is ignorance to not want to know your own Creator. Getting to know the Lord is equal to a person who has a missing parent that they desperately need to know. You need to know your roots, your origin, where you are going, what your life's purpose is. None of this can be accomplished without knowing the Lord. All the truth you need to know is in him. The Lord is not pleased with our lack of knowledge concerning him. He sees our lack of effort in doing so.

In Jeremiah 44:3–5, the Lord said:

> Because of their wickedness which they have committed to provoke me to anger, in that they went to burn incense, and to serve other gods, whom they knew not, neither they, ye, nor your fathers. Howbeit I sent unto you all my servants the prophets, rising early and sending them, saying, oh, do not this abominable thing that I hate. But they hearkened not, nor inclined their ear to turn from their wickedness, to burn no incense unto other gods.

If the Lord says it's wickedness, then it is. Frankly, I'll have to agree with him. How do you forsake a living, breathing God to worship something that is not? "Thus said the Lord; cursed be the man that trusts in man and make flesh his arm and whose heart departs from the Lord" (Jeremiah 17:5). I could never tell you all about the Lord in any one book (or more). I can only encourage you to get to know him. You will not be able to help falling in Love with him. Who is the Lord? His name is Jesus!

It Belongs to God

I have always been fascinated with creative people. I admire those who build things, who capture the awesomeness of God on canvas, who carve something out of wood or stone, who can transform a piece of fabric into the most beautiful clothing or something decorative. However we use the gifted abilities we were born with, we cannot and should not take the credit for any of it.

In Exodus 31:3–4 it says, "I have filled him with the spirit of God, in wisdom, and in understanding and in knowledge to be able to do these things." Philippians 4:13 declares, "I can do all things through Christ which strengthens me." Without God enabling us, we will not be able to.

There is nothing that we build or design that is new to God. In Ecclesiastes 1:9, King Solomon said it all: "There is nothing new under the sun." Psalm 8:3–9 says:

> When I consider thy heavens, the work of thy fingers, the moon and the stars, which though has ordained, what is man that thou art mindful of him? And the son of man that though visits him. For though has made him a little lower than the angels, and has crowned him with glory and honour; thou has made him to have dominion over the works of thy hands; he has put all things under his feet; all sheep and oxen, yes and beasts of the field, the fowl

of the air, and the fish of the seas. O! Lord our Lord,
how excellent is thy name in all the earth!

It is wrong to glorify ourselves for anything we are gifted to
do; neither should we allow anyone to glorify us. All the glory
belongs to God and should never be shifted just because he chose
us as a vessel to bring forth his glory. In Isaiah 40:18, he asked:

> Have you not known, have you not read? Has it
> not been told to you from the beginning? Have
> you not understood from the foundations of
> the earth? It is he that sits upon the circle of the
> earth, and the inhabitants are as grasshoppers;
> that stretches out the heavens as a curtain, and
> spreads them out as a tent to dwell in: that brings
> the princes to nothing: he makes the judges of
> the earth vanity.

The wisdom of God is not to be used to glorify oneself but
rather to be counted as a privilege to share in the plans of the
great and mighty God. I have encountered many people who
praise themselves for their accomplishments in life. They have
not stopped to think that in spite of how gifted they may be, their
gifts would be worthless without the breath of God in them. They
have exalted themselves to the heights of foolishness.

It is tragic to know that we are a people lacking knowledge
when it is available for the taking. We will read every self-
improvement book there is, books to improve one's health, wealth
and attractiveness, but we ignore the book that teaches us how to
live. Not giving God the glory can cost you your life. By the way,
this is not a thing of the past.

King Herod is a prime example of this fact. In Acts 12:22,
Herod basked in the praises of the people without shifting the
glory to God. An angel of the Lord smote him, and he was

eaten of worms. How many of us have been smitten for the same reasons? I wonder. It is the duty of man to worship God and to give him the glory.

Imagine that you have given all you can to your child or children. You've spent your last dime assuring they receive the best education possible. They have now achieved something great in life but have gotten so high minded that they treat you with utter disrespect. How would that make you feel? You may not have thought about it before, but think about it now. How would that make your Father feel?

Here is more food for thought. Let's say that you are an artist who painted an exceptional piece. It is just outstanding. You are very excited about it. You look forward to receiving acknowledgement for all of your hard work. But then someone steals the painting and takes credit for it. This may have never crossed your mind, but think about it. Your Creator is such an artist, and you are his masterpiece.

No matter how great you may think yourself to be, God is greater. If you are being praised for anything, quickly shift it over to God. Any ability, any material, any wisdom, any knowledge that you have was all imported by God. God is fair; he has no problem with you being recognized for the tree you planted as long as you are truthful enough to say the seed came from him. Chapter 12 of Matthew tells the story of the Pharisees who approached Jesus. They asked him if he thought it was right for them to pay taxes. Jesus asked them whose image and superscription was on the penny. They answered that both were Caesar's. Jesus then said, "Give to Caesar what is Caesar's and to God the things which are God's." There is nothing wrong with you getting *credit* for your work, but all the *glory* belongs to God.

Now unto him that is able to keep you from falling
to present you faultless before the presence of his glory
with exceeding joy.
To the only wise God our saviour,
be glory majesty dominion and power,
both now and ever. Amen.
—Jude 1:24–25

Questions for Meditation

Am I living out my true purpose?

If today is my last day, am I truly happy with the way I have lived my life?

Is God truly the center of my life?

What do I need to improve on the most?

What are my biggest obstacles?

Do I fear God or man?

Am I totally free?

Am I walking in love and forgiveness?

TRUE DIRECTIONS

An affiliate of Tarcher Books

OUR MISSION

Tarcher's mission has always been to publish books
that contain great ideas. Why? Because:

GREAT LIVES BEGIN WITH GREAT IDEAS

At Tarcher, we recognize that many talented authors, speakers,
educators, and thought-leaders share this mission and deserve to be
published – many more than Tarcher can reasonably publish ourselves.
True Directions is ideal for authors and books that increase awareness,
raise consciousness, and inspire others to live their ideals and passions.

Like Tarcher, True Directions books are designed to do three things:
inspire, inform, and motivate.

Thus, True Directions is an ideal way for these important voices
to bring their messages of hope, healing, and help to the world.

Every book published by True Directions– whether it is non-
fiction, memoir, novel, poetry or children's book – continues
Tarcher's mission to publish works that bring positive change
in the world. We invite you to join our mission.

For more information, see the True Directions website:
www.iUniverse.com/TrueDirections/SignUp

Be a part of Tarcher's community to bring positive change in this world!
See exclusive author videos, discover new and exciting books, learn about
upcoming events, connect with author blogs and websites, and more!
www.tarcherbooks.com

TRUE DIRECTIONS
AN AFFILIATE OF TARCHER BOOKS

Printed in the United States
By Bookmasters